Number 132
Winter 2011

New Directions for Evaluation

Sandra Mathison
Editor-in-Chief

Internal Evaluation in the 21st Century

Boris B. Volkov
Michelle E. Baron
Editors

INTERNAL EVALUATION IN THE 21ST CENTURY
Boris B. Volkov, Michelle E. Baron (eds.)
New Directions for Evaluation, no. 132
Sandra Mathison, Editor-in-Chief

Microfilm copies of issues and articles are available in 16mm and 35mm, as well as microfiche in 105mm, through University Microfilms Inc., 300 North Zeeb Road, Ann Arbor, MI 48106-1346.

New Directions for Evaluation is indexed in Cambridge Scientific Abstracts (CSA/CIG), Contents Pages in Education (T & F), Higher Education Abstracts (Claremont Graduate University), Social Services Abstracts (CSA/CIG), Sociological Abstracts (CSA/CIG), and Worldwide Political Sciences Abstracts (CSA/CIG).

NEW DIRECTIONS FOR EVALUATION (ISSN 1097-6736, electronic ISSN 1534-875X) is part of The Jossey-Bass Education Series and is published quarterly by Wiley Subscription Services, Inc., A Wiley Company, at Jossey-Bass, One Montgomery Street, Suite 1200, San Francisco, CA 94104-4594.

SUBSCRIPTIONS cost $89 for U.S./Canada/Mexico; $113 international. For institutions, agencies, and libraries, $295 U.S.; $335 Canada/Mexico; $369 international. Prices subject to change.

EDITORIAL CORRESPONDENCE should be addressed to the Editor-in-Chief, Sandra Mathison, University of British Columbia, 2125 Main Mall, Vancouver, BC V6T 1Z4, Canada.

www.josseybass.com

Editorial Policy and Procedures

New Directions for Evaluation, a quarterly sourcebook, is an official publication of the American Evaluation Association. The journal publishes empirical, methodological, and theoretical works on all aspects of evaluation. A reflective approach to evaluation is an essential strand to be woven through every issue. The editors encourage issues that have one of three foci: (1) craft issues that present approaches, methods, or techniques that can be applied in evaluation practice, such as the use of templates, case studies, or survey research; (2) professional issues that present topics of import for the field of evaluation, such as utilization of evaluation or locus of evaluation capacity; (3) societal issues that draw out the implications of intellectual, social, or cultural developments for the field of evaluation, such as the women's movement, communitarianism, or multiculturalism. A wide range of substantive domains is appropriate for *New Directions for Evaluation;* however, the domains must be of interest to a large audience within the field of evaluation. We encourage a diversity of perspectives and experiences within each issue, as well as creative bridges between evaluation and other sectors of our collective lives.

The editors do not consider or publish unsolicited single manuscripts. Each issue of the journal is devoted to a single topic, with contributions solicited, organized, reviewed, and edited by a guest editor. Issues may take any of several forms, such as a series of related chapters, a debate, or a long article followed by brief critical commentaries. In all cases, the proposals must follow a specific format, which can be obtained from the editor-in-chief. These proposals are sent to members of the editorial board and to relevant substantive experts for peer review. The process may result in acceptance, a recommendation to revise and resubmit, or rejection. However, the editors are committed to working constructively with potential guest editors to help them develop acceptable proposals.

Sandra Mathison, Editor-in-Chief
University of British Columbia
2125 Main Mall
Vancouver, BC V6T 1Z4
CANADA
e-mail: nde@eval.org

CONTENTS

Editors' Notes

The growth of internal evaluation is both remarkable and timely. Internal evaluation can be considered a key factor for the overall success of the evaluation field—considering that what happens within an organization is in many ways reflective of the overall attention and trust given to evaluation. Gradually, evaluators and their organizations are bringing evaluative thinking to an internal level, strategically focusing on organizational development and improvement. The internal evaluators are using diverse evaluation tools to conduct evaluations and make their results useful, while at the same time building organizational capacity for integrating evaluation into daily activities.

Given the growing focus on evidence-based policies, organizational accountability, and program improvement, internal evaluation has increasingly become an important subfield, or a specialty area in the field of evaluation. A recent memorandum for the heads of executive departments and agencies from the director of the Office of Management and Budget (OMB), Peter Orszag, is titled "Increased Emphasis on Program Evaluations." The essence of the document is in that, in collaboration with other key agencies, OMB is planning to reconstitute an interagency working group of evaluation experts under the Performance Improvement Council. The objectives of the work group include helping build agency evaluation capacity; creating effective evaluation networks that draw on the best expertise inside and outside the federal government; and sharing best practices from agencies with strong, independent evaluation offices. Agencies are encouraged to propose pertinent changes or reforms and request funding to strengthen their internal evaluation expertise and processes.

This fact and a number of others support the timeliness of this issue. A considerable amount of evaluation work is implemented internally—both nationally and across the world. Other evidence is the considerable number of internal-evaluation–related sessions and presentations offered during the annual conferences of the American Evaluation Association (AEA). The foci of these sessions have taken hold of the field as well—with an emphasis on organizational interrelations, the mainstreaming of evaluation, building evaluation capacity, and creating dynamic evaluation cultures. The heightened interest and activity in the arena of internal evaluation also resulted in the recent formation of the AEA's Internal Evaluation TIG (topical interest group) in 2010, which currently has around 400 members. Also important is the fact that the last—and the only—edition of NDE dedicated to the topic of internal evaluation was published close to three decades ago (see "Developing Effective Internal Evaluation" by Love, 1983). It is a new century now,

NEW DIRECTIONS FOR EVALUATION, no. 132, Winter 2011 © Wiley Periodicals, Inc., and the American Evaluation Association. Published online in Wiley Online Library (wileyonlinelibrary.com) • DOI: 10.1002/ev.391

and a thoughtful discussion about the state of the field of internal evaluation is overdue.

It is in this context that we introduce this issue on internal evaluation. The issue includes evidence-based perspectives on internal evaluation from a number of experienced evaluation practitioners from different fields and organizations, who share practical examples and case studies of their work promoting and conducting internal evaluation in different areas of social programming. The expected readership for this issue is a diverse audience including internal and external evaluators, organization development practitioners interested in program evaluation, and multiple stakeholders who are engaged—or thinking about being engaged—in evaluation and who are sharing commitment to accountability and improvement. This includes professionals in different areas of social programming and specialty evaluation practice (e.g., education, government, and nonprofit).

The issue has the following structure. The first two chapters highlight societal and organizational changes that have influenced the evaluation field and shaped the current trends in internal evaluation. Serving as a springboard for the rest of the issue, Chapter 1 contains an interview by Boris B. Volkov with Arnold J. Love, an internationally recognized internal evaluation expert and author. The choice of the interviewee was by no means accidental. One of the most cited authors on internal evaluation, Arnold J. Love was the editor of the "Developing Effective Internal Evaluation" issue of *New Directions for Program Evaluation*. He shares his experiences and understanding of the development of internal evaluation. Chapter 2 by Sandra Mathison presents an overview of the historical context of internal evaluation from the 1960s to the present, arguing that the growth of the internal evaluation function in organizations has been mainly due to its perceived importance.

The next two chapters are concerned with foundational issues in internal evaluation. Chapter 3 by Boris B. Volkov includes a grounded-in-the-evaluation-literature overview of the essential internal evaluator roles from a macrolevel perspective. The systematic advancing of evaluation capacity, evaluative thinking, and learning in organizations is suggested as one of the future directions for the internal evaluator's progressively changing and expanding roles. In Chapter 4, Francis J. Schweigert focuses on the ethical aspects of the internal evaluation practice. The internal evaluator's ethical promise lies in his or her unique position as a co-worker—within the organization—viewing the organization's work and results with the eye of impartial spectator.

Three more chapters provide rich illustrations of internal evaluation practice in different settings (federal government, public education, military, as well as small organizations) with specific foci (customer-driven vision and a results-based orientation for evaluation, accountability and development, and building evaluation capacity).

In Chapter 5, Ted Kniker addresses the key challenges and opportunities faced by internal government evaluators. His case study is drawn from his experiences as the chief of evaluation for public diplomacy at the U.S. Department of State and as a consultant assisting federal agencies to enhance internal evaluation functions. His internal evaluation office was deemed a best practice by the State Department Office of Inspector General and was recommended to be a model for other U.S. government evaluation units by the Office of Management and Budget.

Chapter 6 by Jean A. King and Johnna A. Rohmer-Hirt discusses the processes of internal evaluation in public education in the United States in general and also illuminates a 10-year reflective case study of internal evaluation in the largest district in Minnesota. The authors believe that the form and viability of internal evaluation is shaped by the unique requirements of the educational sector and that finding resources to sustain meaningful evaluation efforts over time remains a formidable challenge in American public education.

In Chapter 7, Michelle E. Baron presents a case study of her experiences as an inspector general with the military and outlines strategies to develop and maintain internal evaluation systems for small organizations at the early, midterm, and seasoned levels of evaluation capacity. The author believes that internal evaluation can thrive in organizations regardless of their size or resource limitations.

The closing Chapter 8 by Boris B. Volkov and Michelle E. Baron lays out a summary reflection on the key issues and perspectives that emerged in the preceding chapters and other evaluation literature with suggestions for the future directions for internal evaluation research, practice, and training. For example, the directions for practice contain a difficult task of the continuous building of evaluation capacity across the entire organization while cultivating strong independence and credibility of internal evaluation. Collaboration of internal and external evaluators from different organizations, as well as sharing best practices and lessons learned, are among advantageous practices. Future research can benefit the field via identifying an appropriate, comprehensive set of competencies and skills required to be a successful internal evaluator. Such a set could be used in the university and other professional development training to buttress the cadre of the current and aspiring IE practitioners.

The current steady societal movement advocating program accountability, monitoring, and improvement at all organizational levels has significant implications for the entire field of evaluation and for internal evaluation specifically, and will impact both publicly and privately funded programs and organizations. Such a movement makes it exceedingly important for both internal and external evaluators to be aware of the burning issues in conducting evaluation internally and the implications for practice. We hope that this volume will prompt further interest in and research on internal evaluation—with both researchers and communities of practice engaged in dialogue around the issues mentioned in this volume and beyond.

Reference

Love, A.J. (Ed.). (1983). Developing effective internal evaluation [Special issue]. *New Directions for Program Evaluation, 20.*

Boris B.Volkov
Michelle E. Baron
Editors

BORIS B. VOLKOV is an assistant professor of evaluation studies with the Center for Rural Health and Department of Family and Community Medicine at the University of North Dakota School of Medicine and Health Sciences.

MICHELLE E. BARON is an independent evaluation strategist based in Arlington, Virginia.

NEW DIRECTIONS FOR EVALUATION • DOI: 10.1002/ev

Volkov, B. B. (2011). Internal evaluation a quarter-century later: A conversation with Arnold J. Love. In B. B. Volkov & M. E. Baron (Eds.), *Internal evaluation in the 21st century. New Directions for Evaluation, 132,* 5–12.

1

Internal Evaluation a Quarter-Century Later: A Conversation With Arnold J. Love

Boris B. Volkov

Abstract

This chapter features a recent conversation with Dr. Arnold J. Love, a long-time proponent of internal evaluation and one of the most cited internal evaluation authors. In 1983, Love edited the first issue of New Directions for Program Evaluation *on the topic of internal evaluation. He is the author of the book* Internal Evaluation: Building Organizations from Within *(1991), editor of a special issue of the* Canadian Journal of Program Evaluation *about internal evaluation, and the author of a chapter on internal evaluation in* Encyclopedia of Evaluation *(2005). Currently working as an independent evaluation consultant, Love has more than 25 years of experience in evaluation. Based in Toronto, Canada, but also a founding member of the American Evaluation Association, he also brings an important international perspective to our discussion of the status of internal evaluation.* © Wiley Periodicals, Inc., and the American Evaluation Association.

BORIS VOLKOV: Arnold, I would like to start our conversation by thanking you for your willingness to share your thoughts in this *New Directions for Evaluation* issue and by asking you about your personal story of being involved with internal evaluation.

ARNOLD LOVE: It is my great pleasure to speak with you, Boris, about a topic so close to the heart of my career as an evaluator. Before I answer your question, I would like to set the record straight about my position regarding internal evaluation. Because my name is associated so closely with internal evaluation, there is often the misperception that I am promoting internal evaluation as the preferred alternative to external evaluation. Nothing could be further from my own position. I feel that internal evaluation is a valuable form of evaluation, but the choice of any particular form (internal or external) depends on the purpose for the evaluation and a careful consideration of who is in the best position to conduct the evaluation. In some cases it is internal evaluators, but in other cases it is external evaluators.

In terms of my own story, in graduate school I developed an interest in applied research, especially assessing the effectiveness of public and non-profit policies and programs. The term *evaluation research* was just being coined to describe this form of research, primarily the application of rigorous research methodology to the assessment of the process and outcomes of programs. I was fortunate that I learned a wide range of research and measurement approaches, including quantitative methods and qualitative approaches, behavioral analysis and scale construction, complex systems and organizational analyses, and European phenomenological investigation.

To keep the story short, I was hired by a large multiservice agency in Toronto that wanted to build evaluation capacity into their organization. I was very fortunate that the executive director and senior staff practiced leading-edge management approaches that were very much in line with Aaron Wildavsky's concept of "self-evaluating organizations." One of Wildavsky's ideas was that internal evaluation was a key way for organizations to set their own directions, foster change, and know if they were achieving results. So when I saw the notice in a journal that an Evaluation Research Society (ERS) was being formed in the USA, I eagerly attended the first meetings. At those meetings I met kindred spirits—in fact, the Canadian Evaluation Society (CES) began its life as a chapter of the ERS. A few years later, we formed the CES and then provincial chapters. The regional structure of CES encouraged working groups on various topics (similar to AEA's TIG structure), including the interests of internal evaluators.

This was an important step forward, because internal evaluation usually was not seen to be legitimate evaluation at all. A practical consequence was that internal evaluators were generally excluded from conferences, meetings, and conversations with other people who considered themselves to be "real" evaluators. In my experience, the situation was more critical in the United States. There the evaluation field was heavily populated by doctoral-level academics and consultants who were external evaluators. They defined the field. In Canada, on the other hand, the average evaluator held a master's degree and tended to work for government, nonprofit organizations, or for private-sector organizations. In both countries, however, many internal evaluators often carried only part-time evaluation responsibilities, lacked doctoral degrees, and conducted evaluations that served the limited purposes of their organizations. In working with my colleagues and attending evaluation

NEW DIRECTIONS FOR EVALUATION • DOI: 10.1002/ev

conferences, I was confronted by a paradox: It seemed that many more evaluators were doing internal evaluations, but their needs were ignored. Little was known about doing evaluation effectively within organizations. In a nutshell, that is how I came to become a student of internal evaluation.

BORIS VOLKOV: It is hard to quantify the scope of internal evaluation's growth; however, we know that it is on the rise in the U.S. and across the world. What is your perception of the contemporary history of internal evaluation?

ARNOLD LOVE: International surveys and estimates by those who study internal evaluation show considerable variation across countries and cultures. In Canada, at the time that the Canadian Evaluation Society was formed in the late 1970s, our federal government deliberately decided that internal evaluation would be a major model for evaluation. The Royal Commission on Government Organization recommended that government "should be run more like a business" by adopting methods that proved effective in the private sector. Under the slogan "Let the managers manage!" internal evaluation addressed the need for accountability together with systematic program development and quality improvement. Without in-house evaluation and evaluators who were subject-matter experts, there was the fear that reforming government and controlling expenditures was like "conducting an operation on a man carrying a piano upstairs." As you can see, the focus on organizational reform and learning in Canada meant that internal evaluation was not only accepted, but it was promoted as an important form of evaluation.

The history in the U.S. is quite different. In my mind, the watershed point was that infamous "crisis of relevance" in evaluation in the early 1970s. A study commissioned by the Comptroller General's Office concluded that the vast majority of evaluations were not relevant—they took too long, were hamstrung by methodological caveats, reported results long after decisions were made, and were incomprehensible. This report had a dramatic negative impact on the evaluation field and it went into sharp decline. In my opinion, good field research rescued the U.S. evaluation field by carefully examining the small percentage of evaluations that were considered relevant. This led to different approaches to evaluation, such as Michael Q. Patton's utilization-focused evaluation (UFE) model that ensures relevance by building use right into the evaluation process. These new approaches to evaluation gave legitimacy to identifying stakeholders, understanding evaluation needs, participation, selection of appropriate and feasible methods, and the importance of communicating evaluation findings that were already at the heart of the internal evaluation process. I think that the second watershed in the U.S. was the acceptance of internal evaluation as an integral part of the management reforms in the 1980s and 1990s—the notion that evaluation could be a legitimate tool for managing organizations and that organizational learning was as important as accountability. At that point in time, an estimated 60% of the evaluations in the U.S. were internal evaluations and for the next decade that percentage continued to increase.

NEW DIRECTIONS FOR EVALUATION • DOI: 10.1002/ev

In some countries, the percentage is far higher. For example, 5 years ago the Japanese Evaluation Society estimated that 99% of evaluations were internal. This appears to be the situation for most Asian countries, where external evaluation is mistrusted. I find myself in the unusual position of promoting the potential benefits of external evaluation, although my audience cannot imagine how an external evaluator—a perfect stranger, who does not have firsthand knowledge of the program, its politics, its people, its limitations, and its values—can do an evaluation in a relatively short period of time and produce findings that are meaningful to anybody. It is so foreign to cultures which value learning circles or total quality management groups that deeply involve all relevant parties over a long period of time.

In other parts of the world, there is a fair degree of mix between internal and external evaluation. Estimates indicate that some of the northern European countries are least likely to use internal evaluation. This may be traced to their traditional focus on supreme audit organizations where evaluation and auditing are seeing as similar and complementary to each other. Even that situation appears to be changing.

BORIS VOLKOV: More than a quarter-century ago, you wrote: "the notion of the self-evaluating organization that uses program evaluation as the basis for program development and change remains largely an ideal . . ." (Love, 1983, p. 5). What is your current view of the self-evaluating organization? Is it still a dream yet to come true?

ARNOLD LOVE: This vision comes from Aaron Wildavsky (1979), who is best known for his book *Speaking Truth to Power: The Art and Craft of Policy Analysis*. One of his ideas in terms of the self-evaluating organization would be to have people within the organization actively using evaluation information to shape and transform it. Although Wildavsky's dream is not completely realized, it is more a possibility now than ever before. Over the last few decades, we have become much more aware of the way organizations are designed and supported. The advent of affordable computer systems today gives internal evaluators enormous power to collect, analyze, and communicate information. Demands for evaluation from funders, board members, program managers, and partners have made the pressure for evaluation across all sorts of organizations very real, so I believe that we are seeing much more internal evaluation now than in 1983.

In other words, organizations are using evaluation much more, but the second part of Wildavsky's dream of a self-evaluating organization was to have staff that he called "evaluator–manager." In other words, when people became managers, they also had expertise as evaluators and they used that evaluation expertise to actively manage the organization. Over the years, I have taught evaluation to managers of business administration, public administration, and nonprofit administration. I usually teach just one basic graduate course in evaluation to help further the "evaluator–manager" concept. In most MBA programs, there is no training in evaluation whatsoever. Although the pure vision of Wildavsky has not been fully actualized, it's been partially actualized and it has emerged in new varieties, such as networks using evaluation together to learn, and leading-edge practitioners and theorists of evaluation are engaged in that today.

BORIS VOLKOV: Some evaluation pundits insist that practicing internal evaluation in organizations presents unique ethical dilemmas. What major ethical issues do you think should be recognized and how can they be dealt with when practicing internal evaluation?

ARNOLD LOVE: The number one issue is the credibility of internal evaluation. To improve the credibility, you have to reduce the perception that internal evaluation is biased evaluation. Everyone recognizes that when someone is an employee of an organization there may be pressures, subtle or not, to report the desired results. In my internal evaluation courses, I educate evaluators about a variety of proven strategies for reducing bias and increasing the credibility of internal evaluation. For example, one is to apply the AEA Program Evaluation Standards and ethical guidelines so that internal evaluators and their internal clients know them, subscribe to them, and practice them. Another strategy is to have a periodic expert review by an external evaluator(s) to review a sample of internal evaluation studies and give feedback about their quality and potential areas where bias could be an issue. Another strategy is having an evaluation steering committee guide the evaluation, even for internal evaluation. You might include a client representative or student or parent representative if it is in education, as well as perhaps someone from a partner organization who is at arm's length. It gives, in other words, additional eyes and ears to ensure that some issues around credibility and potential bias are being addressed.

The last issue concerns where the evaluation unit is located structurally in an organization. The higher in the organization the evaluation unit is located, the more it is perceived to be independent. Again, the ideal is that the evaluation unit would report directly to the CEO or executive director of the organization, and, if not to that person, to a senior vice-president of the organization. Below that in the organization, internal evaluation is seen as subject to the pressures of managers and colleagues. Likewise, if there is a problem that you identify in an organization, by reporting to the highest level you are in a much better position to shape change.

BORIS VOLKOV: You have been busy working as an independent evaluation consultant internationally. What is your perception of the differences between the ways internal evaluation is practiced in North America and in the rest of the world?

ARNOLD LOVE: In Europe, for example, there is great interest in doing cross-cutting evaluations. These are evaluations that cut across more than one jurisdiction and operate at more than one level. In Europe, they are called "transversal evaluation." For example, the evaluation may look at the effects of a particular employment scheme on an economic zone rather than on a particular country. An economic zone could cover a number of regions that cut across several different countries and multiple levels. Therefore, doing internal evaluation in that environment where you are looking at different levels of entities and organizations is, of course, much more demanding. Yet it is very critical. In Canada we call them "horizontal evaluation," because we often have federal policies that provide the money but then it is up to the provinces to implement (similar to U.S. federal–state programs). There is a demand to see if the national goals are being achieved but also to verify that the common goals across jurisdictions are being accomplished. To do these evaluations well requires a combination of internal and external evaluators. The core group is usually internal evaluators who then follow a rigorous procurement process to hire external evaluators. The external evaluators add the credibility component and also have the technical skills to deal with some of the complexities of the evaluation. In other parts of the world, where the model is primarily internal evaluation, their challenge is how to introduce external evaluation to balance the internal perspective. With solely internal perspective, the danger is that no one can question the fundamental assumptions or drive change.

In the developing world, such as Africa, Central Asia, or South America, for example, much of the internal evaluation work is done at the grassroots level, e.g., community-based organizations, cooperatives with farmers, and scientific organizations that are working in the agriculture or health fields. In these environments, you see a strong desire to build capacity in evaluation to support grassroots efforts and democratic institutions. There are some developments that we would do well to emulate. For example, in Central and South America, universities are cooperating to pool their resources and offer online training for internal evaluators. Nongovernmental organizations are doing the same thing in Africa. They are offering online training for people at the grassroots level who are going to be part-time internal evaluators or internal evaluators working with small groups. As you can see, there are many different models and exciting developments that are going on around the world in internal evaluation.

BORIS VOLKOV: Nowadays, what values and associated training of evaluators are necessary to realize the potential of internal evaluation?

ARNOLD LOVE: The big difference is that the type of evaluation I was talking about in 1983 was very different from the evaluations that we had up until a few years ago. Evaluations were "methods based" and the values of the evaluator were very much focused on the technical side of things, particularly on some variant of a randomized-control trial (RCT). Evaluation was largely top down and the evaluators were technical experts, so they demanded that the programs cooperate with them to collect data according to whatever regime was required for an RCT experiment. We know from evaluation history that this approach to evaluation produced massive resistance and ended up clashing very strongly with the values of the people and the programs. The major change in values has been a focus on utilization. All you have to do is to look at the AEA Standards and Principles for

Evaluators. Both of them talk so much about utilization, about ethics, about using the right technique, and avoiding methods overkill. With a little, tiny program, you do not need to foist a massive evaluation design on people. Internal evaluators try very hard to work with program people rather than against program people, share the values that the people running the programs have, and also respect them and their information needs.

There was little formal training of evaluators, especially training people inside organizations. External evaluators usually had a Ph.D. in applied research, primarily psychology or education, and then they learned on the job. Over the last few decades, we've seen the number of university programs grow but they are still absolutely inadequate. As I recall from several AEA-sponsored surveys, I think that the high point in the U.S. was reached about 15 years ago with 40 universities offering a program in evaluation. In the rest of the world, the situation was far worse. In Canada, we have several universities that offer a graduate degree in evaluation, although there is a proposed abbreviated degree geared to internal evaluators that may be launched soon by a consortium of universities. In Europe, there are a few. Evaluators talk a great deal about evaluation capacity building within organizations, yet the evaluation world has really not done a great job in building that capacity among evaluators. Even so, the situation is much better today than before, thanks to the professional evaluation societies and Evaluators' Institute and the AEA Summer Institute in the U.S., as well as the Essential Skills series (very basic, 1 week's worth of training) in Canada. At least now people working in organizations have more opportunities to learn about evaluation. That part still remains limited, although there is much more talk about it and evaluation capacity building is active in some organizations.

In other parts of the world, for example, in Japan, the Japanese Evaluation Society and the Japanese government work together to develop internal evaluation capacity so that every school has several teachers who can do internal evaluation. About 5 years ago, they started up a program to certify evaluators in the school system. In Canada, CES is beginning a process of credentialing evaluators and that might also stimulate the development of internal evaluation capacity.

BORIS VOLKOV: Almost three decades ago, you predicted that "[d]uring the next few years, we can expect the growth and change in the internal evaluation function to continue" (Love, 1983, p. 20). . .

ARNOLD LOVE: And that happened then. It grew tremendously, so that a few years later and by the 1990s, a great deal of internal evaluation was a reality. My view is that internal evaluation was very much part of the organizational transformations that were going on at the time.

BORIS VOLKOV: Are you still optimistic about the field of internal evaluation? What does your magic ball say about the future trends in this area?

ARNOLD LOVE: Rather than a magic ball, I track the job ads for internal evaluators and I see a steady demand for internal evaluation, without a doubt. The focus on customer- or citizen-driven services and getting customer feedback is still here. To measure and benchmark the quality of services is still here. To strengthen the governance of organizations by having data available to them is there in a very big way. Strategic planning and risk management, both of those things remain essential. Collaborations, partnerships, networks, and the need to have information to keep that whole process going are front and center. Now, a real difference from 1983 is that there is legislation and formal requirements by funding bodies for both evaluation and performance measurement. To do this work well, you need not only external evaluators, but also you need to have strong internal evaluation units to work effectively with external evaluators in order to achieve the formal, legislative requirements for evaluation and reporting.

Organizational learning and change is another important aspect of internal evaluation, and that is still with us. From what I can see, the major reforms over the last decade or so are still with us. They have never been fully implemented and, therefore, the demand is there for internal evaluation. When I look just at job ads, there are many job ads for internal evaluators. I see that as a thriving market. Therefore, if the demand is there then I am optimistic. I think that internal evaluation is now part of the evaluation landscape. My main concern is that most evaluators in general do not have a formal training in finance, in accounting, in budgeting. These days, evaluators need to be able to cost a process or an outcome. Evaluators really should be able to analyze cost effectiveness from the point of view of consumer, citizen, or client outcomes.

References

Love, A. J. (1983). The organizational context and the development of internal evaluation. In A. J. Love (Ed.), Developing effective internal evaluation. New Directions for Program Evaluation, 20, 5–22.

Love, A. J. (1993). Special issue: Internal evaluation. Canadian Journal of Program Evaluation, 8(2).

Wildavsky, A. (1979). Speaking truth to power: The art and craft of policy analysis. Boston, MA: Little, Brown & Co.

BORIS B. VOLKOV is an assistant professor of evaluation studies with the Center for Rural Health and Department of Family and Community Medicine at the University of North Dakota School of Medicine and Health Sciences.

Mathison, S. (2011). Internal evaluation, historically speaking. In B. B. Volkov & M. E. Baron (Eds.), *Internal evaluation in the 21st century. New Directions for Evaluation, 132,* 13–23.

2

Internal Evaluation, Historically Speaking

Sandra Mathison

Abstract

The author analyzes the growth and nature of internal evaluation from the 1960s to the present and suggests that internal evaluation has been on the increase because of its perceived importance. Although the 1960s were characterized by a rich intellectual development of evaluation theory and practice, the fiscal conservatism of the 1980s ushered in evaluation practice focused more specifically on cost effectiveness. During that time, internal evaluation began to increase. In the 1990s this trend continued and was intensified by the reinvention of government known as the New Public Management. The author argues that in this results-oriented neoliberal context, evaluation is maintained as an internal function, but focuses primarily on descriptive accounts of performance. The chapter concludes with some speculation about the nature of future internal evaluation. © Wiley Periodicals, Inc., and the American Evaluation Association.

The magnitude and growth of internal evaluation is difficult to estimate, but anecdotally we have a sense that internal evaluation has become more commonplace, perhaps even the norm. Regrettably, there are no studies that give good evidence about the magnitude of internal evaluation, but informal discussions with evaluators around the world suggest reasonable estimates of evaluation work done internally are: in Australia 80%, in Canada 75%, in France 75%, in the United Kingdom 50%, and in the United States 50%. The expansion of internal evaluation over the last half century can be connected to three distinct stages in developing the role evaluation plays in the public sector. In the 1960s, a period of expansion in evaluation theory and practice, program evaluation was a key means for determining the value and quality of public-sector programming, especially social welfare initiatives. This period saw evaluation become a profession. In the 1980s, this expansive focus gave way to using evaluation to determine the effectiveness and efficiency of social welfare initiatives in a time of shrinking resources. The focus shifted from quality to cost-effectiveness. Finally, a third shift occurred in the 1990s as the New Public Management (NPM) became the organizing strategy for funding and delivering social programming. A key manifestation of NPM in the United States was the 1993 passage of the Government Performance and Results Act (GPRA), legislation that requires federal agencies to develop strategic plans describing their overall goals and objectives, annual performance plans containing quantifiable measures of their progress, and performance reports describing their success. The amount of evaluation done internally has increased with each of these three stages, in part because of the perceived importance of evaluation (House, 1986).

This chapter will discuss each of these evolutionary stages in more detail, including the politics that influence both the move to more internal evaluation and the nature of evaluation practice. (For a very short history of evaluation see Shadish, 2004; for a more detailed account of the evolution of evaluation theory and practice see Shadish, Cook, & Leviton, 1991; and for a history of educational evaluation see Mathison, 2009.)

The 1960s and the Expansion of Evaluation Practice

In the 1960s, a period of expansion in evaluation theory and practice, program evaluation was one of the key means for determining the value and quality of public sector programming, especially social welfare initiatives. Although evaluation is an ancient practice and fundamental to human problem solving, formal and systematic evaluation was bolstered by the infusion of public funding that began with Franklin Roosevelt's New Deal social programs, continued after World War II, and into the 1960s with Lyndon Johnson's Great Society programs. During the 1960s the government took on unprecedented responsibility for the public's welfare, especially in education, housing, and health care.

During the 1960s evaluation practice flourished as federal government officials, elected and appointed, wondered if money for social programs was being well spent and if these social programs accomplished what was expected. Legislation mandating the evaluation of social programs was passed and although this trajectory is not easily mapped, "[e]arly federal programs to require evaluation included the juvenile delinquency program and the Manpower Development and Training Act, both in 1962; the Economic Opportunity Act of 1964; and the Title I (compensatory education) section of the Elementary and Secondary Education Act" (Shadish, 2004, p. 183).

NEW DIRECTIONS FOR EVALUATION • DOI: 10.1002/ev

This demand for program evaluation could not be met by the existing public sector, either in terms of personnel or evaluation knowledge and skills, and private contract firms (for example, Abt Associates, which was created in 1965 by Clark Abt, an engineer, and Westat, which was created in 1963 primarily to provide research and evaluation services to U.S. government agencies) and university-based researchers were the primary source of evaluation expertise. Most program evaluation was contracted out. And the significant involvement of university-based researchers/evaluators contributed to the richness of evaluation theory and practice as professors and graduate students explored and stretched the technical and theoretical limits of social program evaluation.

The 1980s and Evaluation for Efficiency and Cost-Effectiveness

In the 1980s, this focus on exploring and expanding program evaluation gave way to using evaluation to determine the effectiveness and efficiency of social welfare initiatives in a time of shrinking resources. This period of social and fiscal conservatism was marked by skepticism about the value of government-funded social programs and severe cutbacks in federal funding by Republican presidents Ronald Reagan and George H. W. Bush. The focus of evaluations shifted from quality to cost-effectiveness, and from the early 1980s onward internal evaluation begins to appear in the literature as a particular kind of evaluation that could serve these needs (Love, 1983; Sonnichsen & Schick, 1986).

The expansion of evaluation theory and practice from the 1960s onward signaled the potential value of program evaluation for helping policy makers and the public to determine the value of programs in a variety of ways. And with an emphasis on demonstrating cost-effectiveness for program survival, evaluation became a valuable commodity. "Administrators find evaluation too valuable to be left to outside agencies and too dangerous to be removed from administrative control" (House, 1986, p. 63). Arnold Love, Richard Sonnichsen, David Nevo, and I are key authors whose work pointed to the expansion of internal evaluation and the differences and similarities between internal and external evaluation.

In reality, the cost-effectiveness move in evaluation began in the 1960s with the influence of economists and system analysts, people like Alice Rivlin, who saw federally funded programs, like the Elementary and Secondary Education Act, as planned variations or opportunities to examine how new programs stacked up against existing practices in education, housing, job training, and so on. House (1978) called this "evaluation as scientific management" in his analysis of evaluation and educational reform of the time. For Alice Rivlin, who would in time become the Director of the Congressional Budget Office, a key concern in evaluation was the question of which alternative programs produced which benefits and, particularly, which programs provided services most efficiently. Situated squarely within free-market assumptions, the key question for evaluation became one of deciding how to use scarce resources to maximum benefit.

That cost-effectiveness was perceived to be a desirable framework for evaluation does not, however, mean the hope was fully realized. In his discussion of the impact of cost-effectiveness and cost–benefit analysis, Levin (1987, 2001) bemoans the rather modest use of these approaches, which he attributes largely to evaluators' lack of knowledge and decision makers' lack of demand for this type of evaluation.

Internal Evaluation and Decision Making

A notion that solidified during this time was that internal evaluation (indeed all evaluation) ought to serve the interests of governmental and organizational policy makers and managers. Decision-making-oriented evaluation approaches have been dominant in internal evaluation; some evaluation scholars have promoted this orientation for enhancing organizational effectiveness (Love, 1983; Sonnichsen, 2000; Sonnichsen & Schick, 1986), whereas others have critiqued this orientation for its overemphasis on managerial interests and concomitant underemphasis on the interests of other stakeholders (Mathison, 1991a; Scriven, 2002).

"The hallmark of internal evaluation is the systematic use of evaluative information for decision making," so says Love (1983, p. 12). Chelimsky (1987) echoes this view in her discussion of the political framework of the General Accounting Office (GAO) evaluations:

> . . . the choice of the program to evaluate emerges *in real terms* from the political process, with the determination of the types of policy questions to be asked a function of the decision-makers, whether legislative, executive, or both... As such, this framework involves both an empowering of the decision-maker and a shift in the role of the evaluators from the political one of seeking to reform society . . . to the scientific role of bringing the best possible information to bear on a wide variety of policy questions. (p. 202)

Other writers focused on the situatedness of internal evaluators within organizational contexts and the ways in which evaluation practice was influenced when evaluators worked within organizations. The literature during this time demonstrates the realization that what internal evaluators do and whose interests they serve are significantly defined by the organization (Kennedy, 1983); that these organizational contexts are complex, buffeting evaluators back and forth among various, often contradictory, roles (Mathison, 1991b); and that there are multiple possibilities for forms of engagement as internal evaluators (Torres, 1991).

The 1990s and the New Public Management Influence on Evaluation

The interest in efficiency and effectiveness was manifest in the many management strategies for planning and budgeting that began emerging in the

1960s, strategies like management by objectives (MBO), program planning and budget system (PPBS), and zero-based budgeting (ZBB). But a third shift occurred in the 1990s as neoliberalism forged a new relationship between governments, corporations, and the public. Unlike traditional liberalism, which rejects governments in favor of free markets, neoliberalism accepts that there is a necessary role for governments and that role is to facilitate, through policies and practices, capitalist and free-market conditions. New Public Management (NPM), a management philosophy that is meant to modernize the public sector by adopting a market orientation focusing on tangible outcomes and presumably leading to greater cost-efficiency, became the organizing strategy for funding and delivering social programming (Boston, Martin, Pallot, & Walsh, 1996; Pollitt, 1993). Hood (1995, pp. 95–97) summarizes the key features of NPM as

1. disaggregating public services into corporate-like entities,
2. competitive contract-based services, with clear time limits,
3. emphasis on private-sector personnel management,
4. emphasis on the bottom line,
5. accountability through formal indicators and measures of success, and
6. emphasis on outputs.

   A key manifestation of NPM in the United States was the 1993 passage of the GPRA, legislation that requires federal agencies to develop strategic plans describing their overall goals and objectives, annual performance plans containing quantifiable measures of their progress, and performance reports describing their success. The key idea in NPM and manifest in GPRA (although evident in some form in most Organization for Economic Co-operation and Development [OECD] countries) is that of performance measurement. Performance measurement requires the use of a relatively small number of consistent and common benchmarks to indicate the economy, efficiency, and/or effectiveness of a program, activity, or organization.

   Newcomer (1997) argues that program evaluation is a more encompassing practice than performance measurement and that the two ought to be complementary, and suggests evaluators must make the effort to facilitate performance measurement and narrow the conceptual gap between the two (Scheirer & Newcomer, 2001). Although NPM asserts a need for greater involvement of citizens in determining the success of publicly funded programs, performance measurement often reinforces the connection between evaluation and the information needs of program managers, both governmental and nonprofit (see, for example, McDavid & Hawthorn, 2006). Indeed, performance measures are typically chosen by those internal to the organization or agency, so even if an agency has no clearly identified internal evaluation unit, the focus of the evaluation is internally controlled (Langbein, 2006).

Early assessments of the impact of GPRA on federal internal evaluation suggested there was: "(1) little change or a decrease in evaluation activity, authority, funding and staffing; (2) little change in evaluation flexibility and privatization; and (3) an increase in customer focus. In short, the one positive impact—an increase in evaluation customer focus—was overwhelmed by the erosion of government capacity to conduct evaluations during the first year of government reinvention" (Wargo, 1995, p. 236). These early assessments of the impact of GPRA were moderated in 2002 when the Office of Management and Budget created the Program Assessment Rating Tool (PART). The Government Accountability Office's (GAO's) evaluation of GPRA indicates that with the implementation of PART there was a dramatic increase in the availability of performance data (U.S. GAO, 2004), but also reported that "we have not observed notable increases in federal managers' perceptions about their personal use of plans or performance information when allocating resources, or about the use of performance information when funding decisions are made about their programs" (p. 100). Even if not entirely successful, the emphasis on coupling decision making and performance measurement has created an internal evaluation process that is meant to serve decision-making and decision makers.

Arguably, the impact of NPM, at least in the United States, has been a siphoning of internal evaluation resources (and perhaps also programming resources) to create and manage information systems that enumerate goals and describe progress toward those goals. The GAO's evaluation of GPRA notes, however, there is often too little attention paid to evaluation, the sort of strong analysis that extends beyond the descriptive nature of performance measurement. Consistent with this is Davies' (1999) observation across many national governments that performance management is more pervasive, pushing aside evaluation as it might have been conceived in the 1960s.

The Potential Contradictory Consequences of NPM on Program Evaluation

NPM can potentially create contradictory consequences on the balance of internal and external evaluation within the public sector. On the one hand, NPM values internal evaluation, albeit in the form of monitoring and accountability, whereas on the other hand, NPM also promotes the contracting out of services, one of which may be evaluation. An example of the former is the GAO and an example of the latter is the What Works Clearinghouse within the U.S. Department of Education.

Staying in Control, Keeping Evaluation Close

Being held accountable for performance standards and specific outcomes seems logical, but is also risky enough that maintaining control over the evaluation is a desirable strategy. As already suggested, the U.S. General

Accounting Office is perhaps the best example of a government's maintaining an internal evaluation unit. However, the federal government does not have the resources to do all evaluation, and so responsibility to do evaluation is devolved to the local level but is constrained by goals, priorities, and outcomes established at a centralized level—the very essence of outcomes-based accountability.

But with the disaggregation of public services supported by NPM, local control over the evaluation provides some assurance that local policy and decision makers maintain control over programming and the representation of their success. A good example of this is the U.S. federal control of education through the accountability requirements outlined in the No Child Left Behind legislation. However, state departments of education maintain control over much of the actual assessment and reporting that demonstrates their performance, which in turn permits the adjustment of standards to meet the federal accountability demands.

Contracting Out Evaluation, Capitalizing on the Work of Others

NPM favors contracts, especially in the name of efficiency and with terms that allow for the discontinuation of the contract should the services no longer be required or deemed poor quality. Rather than having civil servants conducting evaluation within an internal evaluation unit, evaluation might also be contracted out. An excellent example of the U.S. government's use of this logic, while still maintaining control of what is considered good evaluation, is the What Works Clearinghouse (WWC). With fewer resources available to fund educational evaluation, the U.S. Department of Education has turned its attention via the WWC to research and evaluation. The WWC intends to promote informed education decision making by building easily accessible databases and reports that provide education consumers with reviews of the effectiveness of replicable educational interventions (programs, products, practices, and policies). What is key is that these evaluations are not commissioned, funded, or monitored by the federal government. Staff of the WWC accept nominations for studies that might be included, as well as trolling the literature for additional possibilities.

"Is Internal or External Evaluation Better?" Is the Wrong Question

Although it is not the purpose of this chapter to discuss internal evaluation in relation to external evaluation, it bears noting that an often-false choice is created in much of the literature on internal evaluation. Asking whether one or the other is better is not a question that can be answered generically. Internal and external evaluations are different and decisions about which approach makes sense are not a matter of adherence to some criteria that necessarily identify one over the other as most desirable. Discussions in the

**Figure 2.1. Five Suggested Pathways for Combining Internal and
External Evaluation**

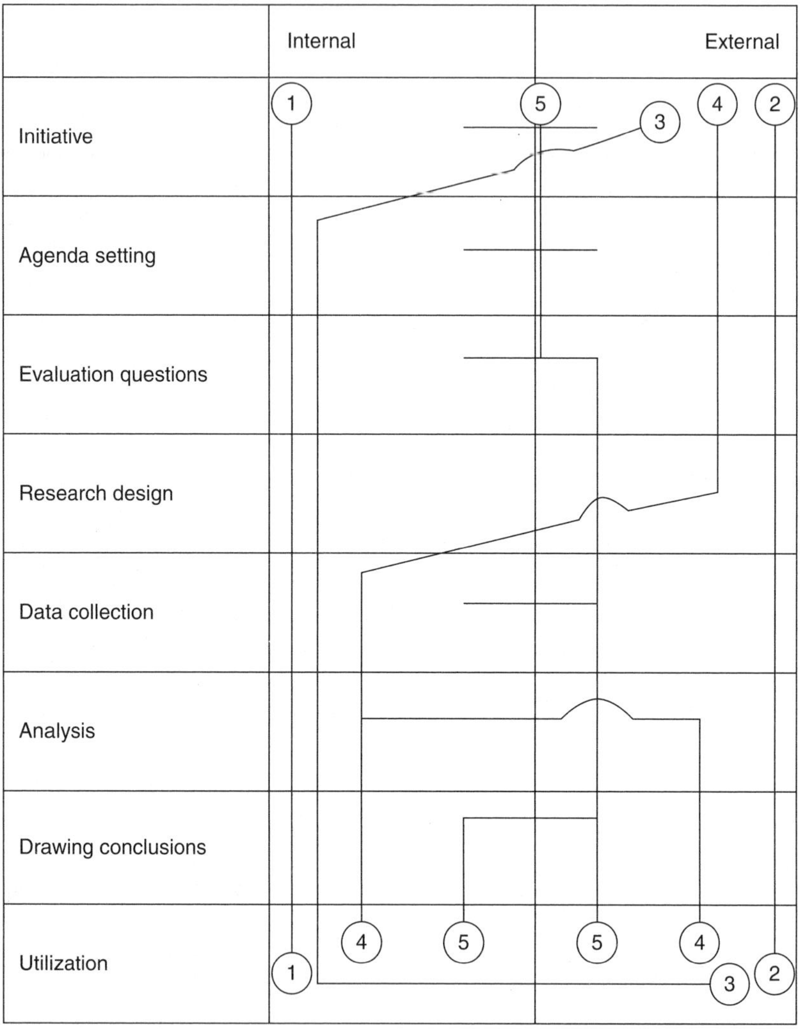

Source: Dahler-Larsen (2009).

past decade, especially among European evaluators, suggest fostering complementary and mutually beneficial relationships between internal and external evaluations and evaluators (Christie, Ross, & Klein, 2004; Dahler-Larsen, 2009; Nevo, 2001; VanHoof & Van Petegem, 2007; Watling & Arlow, 2002). Figure 2.1 illustrates Dahler-Larsen's useful conceptualization of at least five pathways for combining internal and external evaluation.

NEW DIRECTIONS FOR EVALUATION • DOI: 10.1002/ev

Future Trends for Internal Evaluation

If evaluation blossomed as a discipline and profession in the 1960s, became more focused on cost effectiveness in the 1980s, and became a handmaiden to the reinventing of government and the public sector that spread across the globe in the 1990s, where is evaluation going from here? And, more specifically, what does internal evaluation look like in the future?

Love (2005, p. 207) described trends for internal evaluation, trends that suggest targeted, nimble evaluation that still focuses on the fundamental values of NPM:

> Replacing "wall to wall" evaluations that review all programs with monitoring systems to identify "hot spots" that require in-depth evaluations
>
> Shifting from large databases to smaller program-level "data marts" and distributed networks with rapid access to information, which encourages the strategic use of information and a quick response to changing conditions
>
> Replacing written evaluation reports with new reporting formats designed to provide information when it is really needed, such as writing letters to flag a concern, having evaluators sit on program committees, and holding a wrap-up session rather than writing a final report
>
> Working with managers, staff, and clients to articulate clear outcomes and developing tools for measuring the outcomes and best practices that contribute value for money.

Not surprisingly, internal evaluation has also been linked to the idea of learning organizations (Love, 1991; Minnett, 1999; Sonnichsen, 2000). Internal evaluators who have close working relationships with other organizational members are seen as advocates for positive change within their organizational contexts.

Others suggest that NPM has given way to digital-era governance, a shift that "involves reintegrating functions into the governmental sphere, adopting holistic and needs-oriented structures, and progressing digitalization of administrative processes" (Dunleavy, Margetts, Bastow, & Tinkler, 2006, p. 467). The changes in information technology suggest we are entering a new era for evaluation in general, and internal evaluation in particular. The development of electronic health records, for example, has the dual purposes of facilitating quality patient care and judging the quality of that same patient care. Internal evaluators may well be responsible for the creation of electronic databases, information management systems, data warehousing, and the strategies for mining these to answer specific evaluation questions. And, the concomitant e-service delivery plans and open engagement tactics of many governments suggest new ways for evaluators to judge the value of service provision. As Love (2005) suggests, the reporting of evaluation findings internally may shift to Web-based strategies, digital presentations, and technology-enhanced real-time communications. If indeed we are entering a digital governance era, the fundamental idea of disaggregation in NPM will necessarily give way to recentralization through information systems.

At least in the United States, the 2010 Modernization of GPRA Act suggests a potential intensification of the internal evaluation function, albeit in the form of performance monitoring that focuses on far fewer goals with results on the accomplishment of those goals more frequently reported. Indeed, there is little to suggest that evaluation will not continue to be subverted by an emphasis on performance management that attempts to narrow the gap between performance measurement and resource and programmatic decision making.

References

Boston, J., Martin, J., Pallot, J., & Walsh, P. (1996). *Public management: The New Zealand model.* Auckland, New Zealand: Oxford University Press.

Chelimsky, E. (1987). What have we learned about the politics of program evaluation? *Educational Evaluation and Policy Analysis, 9*(3), 199–213.

Christie, C. A., Ross, R. M., & Klein, B. M. (2004). Moving toward collaboration by creating a participatory internal-external evaluation team: A case study. *Studies in Educational Evaluation, 30,* 125–134.

Dahler-Larsen, P. (2009). Learning oriented educational evaluation in contemporary society. In K. E. Ryan & J. B. Cousins (Eds.), *The Sage international handbook of educational evaluation.* Thousand Oaks, CA: Sage.

Davies, I. C. (1999). Evaluation and performance management in government. *Evaluation, 5*(2), 150–159.

Dunleavy, P., Margetts, H., Bastow, S., & Tinkler, J. (2006). New public management is dead—long live digital-era governance. *Journal of Public Administration Research and Theory, 16*(3), 467–494.

Hood, C. (1995). The "New Public Management" in the 1980s: Variations on a theme. *Accounting, Organizations and Society, 20*(2/3), 93–109.

House, E. R. (1978). Evaluation as scientific management in U.S. school reform. *Comparative Education Review, 22*(3), 388–401.

House, E. R. (1986). Internal evaluation. *American Journal of Evaluation, 7*(1), 63–64.

Kennedy, M. (1983). The role of the in-house evaluator. *Evaluation Review, 7*(4), 519–541.

Langbein, L. (2006). *Public program evaluation.* Armonk, NY: M. E. Sharpe Inc.

Levin, H. M. (1987, Summer). Cost-benefit and cost-effectiveness analyses. *New Directions for Program Evaluation, 34.*

Levin, H. M. (2001, Summer). Waiting for Godot: Cost-effectiveness analysis in education. *New Directions for Evaluation, 90,* 55–68.

Love, A. (1983). The organizational context and the development of internal evaluation. *New Directions for Program Evaluation, 20,* 5–12.

Love, A. (1991). *Internal evaluation: Building organizations from within.* Newbury Park, CA: Sage.

Love, A. (2005). Internal evaluation. In S. Mathison (Ed.), *Encyclopedia of evaluation.* Thousand Oaks, CA: Sage.

Mathison, S. (1991a). What do we know about internal evaluation? *Evaluation and Program Planning, 14*(3), 159–165.

Mathison, S. (1991b). Role conflicts for internal evaluators. *Evaluation and Program Planning, 14*(3), 173–179.

Mathison, S. (2009). Public good and private interest: A history of educational evaluation. In W. C. Ayers, T. Quinn, & D. Omatoso Stovall (Eds.), *The handbook of social justice in education.* London, United Kingdom: Routledge.

McDavid, J. C., & Hawthorn, L. L. (2006). *Program evaluation and performance measurement.* Thousand Oaks, CA: Sage.

Minnett, A. M. (1999). Internal evaluation in a self-reflective organization: One nonprofit agency's model. *Evaluation and Program Planning, 22*(3), 353–362.

Newcomer, K. E. (1997). Using performance measurement to improve programs. In K. E. Newcomer (Ed.), *New Directions for Evaluation, 75,* 5–14.

Nevo, D. (2001). School evaluation: Internal or external? *Studies in Educational Evaluation, 27,* 95–106.

Pollitt, C. (1993). *Managerialism and the public services* (2nd ed.). Oxford, United Kingdom: Blackwell.

Scheirer, M., & Newcomer, K. E. (2001). Opportunities for program evaluators to facilitate performance-based management. *Evaluation and Program Planning, 24*(1), 63–71.

Scriven, M. (2002). Evaluation ideologies. In D. L. Stufflebeam, G. F. Madaus, & T. Kellaghan (Eds.), *Evaluation models: Viewpoints on educational and human services evaluation.* New York, NY: Springer.

Shadish, W. (2004). History of evaluation. In S. Mathison (Ed.), *Encyclopedia of evaluation.* Newbury Park, CA: Sage.

Shadish, W. R., Cook, T. D., & Leviton, L. C. (1991). *Foundations of program evaluation.* Newbury Park, CA: Sage.

Sonnichsen, R. C. (2000). Effective internal evaluation: An approach to organizational learning. In F. L. Leeuw, R. C. Rist, & R. C. Sonnichsen (Eds.) *Can governments learn?* New Brunswick, NJ: Transaction Publishers.

Sonnichsen, R. C., & Schick, G. A. (1986). Evaluation: A tool for management. *FBI Law Enforcement Bulletin, 55*(2), 5–10.

Torres, R. (1991). Improving the quality of internal evaluation: The evaluator as consultant-mediator. *Evaluation and Program Planning, 14*(3), 189–198.

U.S. Government Accountability Office (2004). *Results-oriented government: GPRA has established a solid foundation for achieving greater results* (GAO Report No. 04–38). Washington, DC: Author.

VanHoof, J., & Van Petegem, P. (2007). Matching internal and external evaluation in an era of accountability and school development: Lessons from a Flemish perspective. *Studies in Educational Evaluation, 33*(2), 101–119.

Wargo, M. J. (1995). The impact of federal government reinvention on federal evaluation activity. *American Journal of Evaluation, 16*(3), 227–237.

Watling, R., & Arlow, M. (2002). Wishful thinking: Lessons from the internal and external evaluations of an innovatory education project in Northern Ireland. *Evaluation & Research in Education, 16*(3), 166–181.

SANDRA MATHISON is a professor of education at the University of British Columbia and the editor-in-chief of New Directions for Evaluation.

3

Beyond Being an Evaluator: The Multiplicity of Roles of the Internal Evaluator

Boris B. Volkov

Abstract

The chapter explores critical roles of internal evaluators in contemporary organizational settings. The need is highlighted for an expanded, reconfigured, unorthodox set of roles and styles of work to meet the needs of the emerging learning organizations effectively. A discussion of major categories of internal evaluator roles emerged from the analysis of the evaluation literature and other sources suggests new directions for how internal evaluation is conceptualized and practiced. Systematic promoting and advancing positive change, evaluation capacity building, decision making, learning, and evaluative thinking in organizations are seen as part of the harmonized internal evaluator role. © Wiley Periodicals, Inc., and the American Evaluation Association.

Given the ever-increasing importance of evaluation information for organizational planning and decision-making processes, as well as the fact that a substantial share of evaluation work nationally and worldwide is implemented internally (Fitzpatrick, Sanders, & Worthen, 2004; Love, 1991, 2005; Sonnichsen, 2000), there is a strong need to develop better understanding of multiple roles and associated practices of internal evaluators. According to Skolits, Morrow, and Burr (2009), descriptions of evaluator roles in the existing literature are in many cases not sufficiently delineated or conceptualized. Chelimsky (2001) makes the point that the roles and responsibilities of the internal evaluators in the organizations ought to be pragmatically clarified.

So far, there is no unanimous agreement on the classification of the effective internal evaluation (IE) practices and associated internal evaluator roles. Only a handful of authors (Love, 1991; Patton, 2008; Sonnichsen, 2000) have tried to capture the gamut of the internal evaluator roles. Even though "carefully defining the role of internal evaluator is a key to effective and credible internal evaluation use" (Patton, 2008, p. 221), there have not been recent publications that would synthesize the existing information on the various roles of internal evaluators. There is a considerable gap in the literature in this area. In an attempt to improve this situation, this chapter utilizes information from an extensive review of the empirical literature on evaluation and evaluation capacity building (ECB) in organizations, the author's personal experiences with implementing and studying internal evaluation and ECB, and other sources.

Defining Internal Evaluation

Internal evaluation has been defined in various ways. The operative terms include *internal, decision-making, information, learning*. Michael Scriven's Evaluation Thesaurus describes IE as that "done by project staff, even if they are special evaluation staff—that is, even if they are external to the production/writing/teaching/service part of the project" (Scriven, 1991, p. 197). There is broad agreement in the internal evaluation literature that IE exists to support the organizational and program management decision-making process (Duffy, 1994; Love, 1983b, 1991; Patton, 2008; Sonnichsen, 2000; Torres, 1991). Duffy (1994) describes IE as the process of using qualified, experienced staff members "to assess their organization's policies, programs, or problems and report their findings and recommendations to the head of the organization" (p. 26). The internal evaluation process in organizations serves "the dual purpose of providing information and of influencing behavior, including decision-making behavior" (Love, 1983b, p. 8). Torres (1991) writes about the traditional view and practice of internal evaluation as "a staff function informing operations, management, and/or strategic planning" (p. 190). According to her, increasingly, the goal of internal evaluation is not about reflecting the perspectives of program management but rather about promoting empathetic and responsible decision making through the fair and sensitive representation of multiple issues and perspectives and based on the use of the evaluative information.

Internal evaluation is also a powerful organizational intervention with the methodology contingent on political and practical circumstances (Love, 1991). Among many other things, internal evaluation can be called an applied research activity in support of organizational development and learning (Love, 2005). Duffy (1994) perceives IE as a variation of "action research, frequently focusing on issues of immediate concern to the management of an organization" (p. 25). This type of applied research draws on a wide assortment of approaches and methodologies from multiple fields (e.g., organizational psychology, the management and information sciences). Sonnichsen (2000) asserts that "internal evaluation is not simply the application of traditional evaluation methodologies inside organizations but the adaptation, reconstruction, and reframing of evaluation methodologies to operate effectively inside organizations" (p. 23).

Based on the literature review and my own experience, I would like to suggest a systems-based understanding of internal evaluation. Internal evaluation can be defined as a comprehensive and context-dependent system of intraorganizational processes and resources for implementing and promoting evaluation activities for the purposes of generating credible and practical knowledge to inform decision making, to make judgments about and improve programs and policies, and to influence organizational learning and decision-making behavior. We will discuss the internal evaluator's roles needed to make such a system operate successfully.

Expanding the Traditional Evaluator Role

The notion of "the 'role of the evaluator' is central to the theory and practice of evaluation" (Ryan & Schwandt, 2002, p. vii). The term *role* is also central to this chapter; therefore, it is important to clarify what it actually means. A role is an explicitly and implicitly expected function performed and behavior associated with a particular position in an organization. Katz and Kahn (1978) perceive a role as a building block of a social system conveying the requirements of that system to its members. Roles are also the translation of professional values, priorities, and principles into behaviors and courses of action to deliver desired results. Internal evaluation work is shaped to a substantial degree by such roles, which provide combinations of behavioral and social expectations for what is effective, appropriate, and meaningful. Evaluators' roles, in turn, are defined, according to Themessl-Huber, Harrow, and Laske (2005), by the competencies they need, the functions they are expected to carry out, how they interrelate with evaluation stakeholders, and the contextual factors presented by the organization or program. Patton (2008) also emphasizes the responsiveness of the role of an evaluator to the circumstances of actual practice.

A number of additional, ostensibly external to evaluation, roles come into play for internal evaluator. Clifford and Sherman (1983) argue that the internal evaluators face pressures and objectives inside organizations that are very different from those of their external colleagues. Internal evaluators have to make appropriate adaptations to fit their roles to particular organizational conditions. Speaking of the proverbial resistance to evaluation in organizations, it is my belief that in many cases it is not an antievaluation sentiment overall, but rather a rejection of bad evaluations and/or evaluators. The "it is not the evaluator's job!" mentality is engrained in some evaluators who neglect the importance of responsiveness, flexibility, and creativity that must be applied to their functions and, as a result, find themselves not being able to do their real job effectively; as a result they are forced to reconsider the nature of their practice. Without adjusting and expanding the evaluators' role kit, the situation may not be much different from the one Love (1983a) lamented about by saying that "the image of the internal evaluator appears to fluctuate between that of a hatchet man for the executive director and that of an emissary from Babel who speaks in a strange tongue about incomprehensible topics" (p. 2).

Considerable evaluation literature underpins the perspective of the expanding of the traditional role of the evaluator (e.g., Anderson-Draper, 2006; Barkley, 2001; Bellavita, Wholey, & Abramson, 1986; Jenlink, 1994; Love, 1983a, 1991; Newman & Brown, 1996; Preskill, 1994). The internal evaluation role in organizations, according to Barkley (2001), is more of "a study in professional cross dressing requiring the adoption of new roles, swapping of disciplines and crossing of boundaries in reconfigured, decentred, organisations that display multiple cross sectoral identities" (p. 2).

The internal evaluator role set is an emergent property, the arising of interdependent patterns and functions during the process of adaptation to the complex, changing world of organizations. It is affected by interactions with the organization leadership, program staff, program beneficiaries, and partners. This allegorical advertisement by Dozois, Langlois, and Blancher-Cohen (2010), listing a range of competencies and capacities for the developmental evaluation practitioner, can be easily translated into a job ad for the internal evaluator:

> Wanted. Caring individuals to support a hazardous but important journey. Must be able to play a variety of roles: coach, strategist, observer, researcher, facilitator, cheerleader, lore keeper, map maker, and critical friend. High tolerance for complexity and uncertainty important. People skills critical. Must be passionate about creating positive social change. (p. 62)

This chapter is concerned with so-called *macrolevel* evaluator roles addressing "higher level orientation to an evaluation" (Skolits et al., 2009, p. 292) as compared to the evaluation activity-based (microlevel) roles suggested by the same authors for external evaluators (also applicable to internal evaluators, in my view) to address responsive role orientations for the specific evaluation activities in which they are often engaged. The two approaches are concordant. It is not a purpose of this article to identify all the roles needed for internal evaluation to be relevant and effective. Internal evaluation is a rather complex undertaking with many potentially important variables and conditions. The objective here is to highlight a limited selection of categories of roles that are currently seen to be of most utility for internal evaluators to be able to influence organizations and their programs positively.

Essential Roles Associated With Internal Evaluation

A quick analysis of the 2010 AEA Career Center listings showed that about 50% of them were strictly internal evaluator positions. The job titles, instead of *evaluation*, could include the words *assessment, measurement, monitoring, learning, knowledge management*, and *accountability*. The internal evaluator job descriptions were up to three pages long and included multiple responsibilities in diverse areas. The range of internal evaluation activities within organizations include, but are not limited to, implementing needs and evaluability assessments; developing program theories/logic models; developing evaluation plans; developing appropriate measures, indicators, methods, and instruments; coordinating, implementing, and training others in data collection, management, and analysis; forming conclusions; providing recommendations and promoting their appropriate use; writing evaluation reports, policy briefs, and fact sheets; presenting to multiple audiences; writing requests for proposals (RFPs) for external evaluation; selecting external evaluators and coordinating their work; and building evaluation capacity in the organization. All of the above activities involve ongoing interaction with multiple stakeholders. In other words, a good internal evaluator ought to be a real jack-of-all-trades.

The findings of the American Evaluation Association's (AEA's) Internal Evaluation Topical Interest Group (IE TIG) membership survey (administered in October 2010) demonstrate that the perceived critical roles played by internal evaluators include designing and implementing evaluations, building evaluation capacity and facilitating evaluations, managing internal evaluation, collecting and analyzing data, analyzing and judging programs, and maintaining monitoring and evaluation (M & E) systems. A number of experiences were also shared by internal evaluation practitioners during a discussion at the IE TIG's inaugural business meeting at the 2010 AEA conference. The meeting participants described their roles and responsibilities as

coaching on data use and helping avoid its misuse as opposed to only providing data,
"selling" services as opposed to "selling" data,
working around evaluation utilization,
showing relevance of evaluation to improving organizational practices,
tying evaluation use into data-driven decision making,
increasing transparency of decisions,
building capacity for evaluation and its use, and
helping/empowering people to become their own evaluators.

This section presents a list of the patterns that emerged in a comprehensive literature analysis of the sources explicitly discussing evaluator roles (see Table 3.1). The list is intended to help us better understand strategic roles driving the evaluation function in the organizations. The most frequently

Table 3.1. Major Categories of the Evaluator Roles Found in the Evaluation Literature

Major Role Category	Examples of Evaluator Roles	Sources/Authors
Change agent	Change agent; agent of social change; activist; promoting social justice, transformation, and democracy; facilitator of deliberative democratic dialogues; contributing to social betterment and transformation; pursuing potentially unpopular issues; discusser of the undiscussables; educator of change processes; critic; critical friend; social critic; whistle-blower	Bellavita, Wholey, and Abramson (1986); Benjamin and Greene (2009); Duffy (1994); Everitt (1996); Greene (2000); House and Howe (1999); Huberty (1982; 1988); King and Stevahn (2002); Mark, Henry, and Julnes (2000); Mathison (1991a); Mertens (2002); Minnett (1999); Newman and Brown (1996); Patton (2008); Preskill and Torres (1999); Rallis and Rossman (2000); Scriven (2007); Segerholm (2002); Sonnichsen (1988; 2000); Weiss (1998); Whitmore (1998)
Educator about evaluation	Educating about evaluation; teaching, training, coaching, mentoring, and providing technical assistance to managers, staff, and other stakeholders; popularization of evaluation; resource for infusing evaluative thinking	Braverman and Arnold (2008); Chelimsky (1994); Christie (2008); Clifford and Sherman (1983); Conley-Tyler (2005); Dahler-Larsen (2006); Lambur (2008); Leviton (2001); Love (1991); Lyle (2000); Mathison (1991a); Minnett (1999); Morabito (2002); Patton (2008); Preskill and Torres (1999); Rennekamp and Engle (2008); Scriven (2001); Shulha and Cousins (1997); Taylor-Powell and Boyd (2008); Williams and Hawkes (2003)
ECB practitioner	Building evaluation capacity; long-term education of the organization; promoting evaluation; infusing evaluative thinking; facilitating learning processes; leadership role in "mainstreaming" evaluation into the organization; building an organization's skills and knowledge; driving force for ECB	Baron (this issue); Braverman and Arnold (2008); Conley-Tyler (2005); Dahler-Larsen (2006); Lambur (2008); Leviton (2001); Love (1991); Patton (2008); Preskill and Torres (1999); Sanders (2002); Rennekamp and Engle (2008); Schweigert (this issue); Sonnichsen (2000); Taylor-Powell and Boyd (2008); Volkov (2008); Williams and Hawkes (2003)

Role	References
(Management) decision-making supporter	Supporting program decision making; management facilitator, analyst, adviser, and consultant; management supporter; management information resource; management decision-support specialist; administrator's tool; problem solver; expert troubleshooter	Brazil (1999); Clifford and Sherman (1983); House (1986); Kennedy (1983); Leviton (2001); Love (1983b, 1991); Mathison (1991b); Patton (2008); Sonnichsen (2000); Stufflebeam (2003); Torres (1991); Weiss (1998); Wholey (1983)
Consultant	Consultant; management consultant; program staff consultant; organizational development consultant; consultant–mediator; advisor or a consultant to program managers; adviser; counselor	Barkdoll (1982); Brazil (1999); Clifford and Sherman (1983); Fleischer (1983); Lambur (2008); Love (1983, 1991); Morabito (2002); Owen and Lambert (1998); Patton (2008); Perrin (2001); Rennekamp and Engle (2008); Sonnichsen (1988, 2000); Torres (1991)
Researcher/technician/analyst	Researcher; applied researcher supporting organizational development and learning; social researcher and operations researcher; social scientist; technical servant; technician; technical geek; collaborative researcher; action researcher; policy analyst, studying topics selected by top management	Brazil (1999); Campbell (1969); Clifford and Sherman (1983); Hopson (2002); Kennedy (1983); Love (2005); Mark (2002); Noblit and Eaker (1987); Skolits et al. (2009); Sonnichsen (1988); Weiss (1998)
Advocate	Program advocate; advocacy for support; champion of evaluation; advocate for intended primary users; evaluation use advocate; advocate for the program's target groups; advocate for the most vulnerable population; advocate for cultural justice	Bellavita, Wholey, and Abramson (1986); Greene (1997); Hood (2001); Hopson (2001); Mertens (2007); Newman and Brown (1996); Patton (2008); Skolits et al. (2009); Sonnichsen (2000); Stake (2004)
Organizational learning promoter	Building, supporting, and promoting organizational learning; organizational development consultant; advancing organizational knowledge; educating about learning and change processes	Braverman and Arnold (2008); Clifford and Sherman (1983); Fleischer (1983); Leviton (2001); Love (2005); Morabito (2002); Owen and Lambert (1998); Preskill and Torres (1999); Russ-Eft and Preskill (2001); Sonnichsen (2000)
Other roles	Facilitator; generalist/jack-of-all-trades; planner; collaborator; independent observer; evaluator; judge; information specialist	Multiple authors

cited categories of roles of the evaluator include change agent, educator about evaluation, ECB practitioner, (management) decision-making supporter, consultant, researcher/technician/analyst, advocate, and organizational learning supporter. In the "other" category can be found such roles as a facilitator, generalist, planner, collaborator, independent observer, judge, information specialist, and last but not least the role of evaluator (which may seem like a tautology). Some of the roles are partly or substantially overlapping roles—complementing and reinforcing each other. Because it is impractical due to space limitations to discuss all categories of roles mentioned in the evaluation literature, this section will highlight only a few roles suggested by the majority of the reviewed literary sources.

Change Agent

The most frequent role mentioned in the literary sources was change agent—and for an obvious reason. We usually evaluate something to make it right, to correct and improve things, in other words, to bring a positive change to what we are doing. According to Sonnichsen (2000), for internal evaluators, change agent is a fundamental role involved with scrutinizing organizational performance and providing recommendations for improvement. A large number of internal evaluators, according to Duffy (1994), consider themselves change agents in their contributing to the formulation of policy development. Capable members of the evaluation unit strategically situated within the organizational hierarchy and functioning within a change agent and advocacy role can contribute to significant organizational learning and transformation.

Internal evaluators maintain their credibility and integrity only when they are not afraid to speak truth to power and to the powerless, to "pursue potentially unpopular issues" (Mathison, 1991b, p. 177), to ask hard questions, and to discuss the undiscussables (Minnett, 1999; Senge, 1997). As a result, positive changes can be brought about in diverse ways and affect different levels within the program, organization, and far beyond. This is the reason why, in addition to evaluation use, Kirkhart (2000) suggests the notion of evaluation influence to describe "the capacity or power of persons or things to produce effects on others by intangible or indirect means" (p. 7). Evaluators should contribute to social betterment and transformation (King & Stevahn, 2002; Mark, Henry, & Julnes, 2000), serve as facilitators of deliberative democratic dialogues (House, 1993; House & Howe, 1999), and support social justice (Greene, 2000; Mertens, 2002).

Educator About Evaluation

The internal evaluator is an educator by design. Education as a role of evaluation in society was emphasized by Cronbach & Associates (1980) and

Weiss (1998). However, according to Mathison (1991b), the internal evaluator is "also an educator about evaluation—about what evaluation is, about what evaluation can and cannot do, about evaluation as an area of intellectual interest. Just because an organization decides it should have its own evaluation office, this is no guarantee of a practical understanding of what evaluation is" (p. 178). Scriven (2001) states that people should be offered adequate education about the value of evaluation. Patton (2008) learned that "people were more receptive to evaluation if they understood it from within their own worldview" and stressed the importance of connecting program staff and participants with "this alien and often fear-inducing notion of evaluation" (p. 103). Similarly, Christie (2008) illuminates the role of the internal evaluator as a teacher who dispels myths about program evaluation.

Indeed, many evaluation practitioners excel at educating a variety of stakeholders about multifaceted aspects of evaluation with the use of a number of techniques. For example, their efforts include dissemination of evaluation results to colleagues and partners; sharing examples of successful evaluation practices that relate to the organization; conducting seminars about evaluation approaches and techniques (Minnett, 1999); or "training managers and employees in quality control methods, quality measurement, and interpersonal techniques" (Love, 1991, p. 79). "Learning by doing it" is another approach, the importance of which is hard to overemphasize (Volkov, 2008; Volkov & King, 2007). It includes the meaningful and persistent engagement of the program stakeholders in evaluation planning, developing logic models, data collection and analysis, and reporting.

ECB Practitioner

The evaluation capacity-building practice is different from program evaluation in that the goal of ECB is to strengthen and sustain effective evaluation practices; however, IE and ECB have strong potential for reinforcing each other in multiple areas and can be coevolving, systematic, and adaptive processes. ECB processes and outcomes can be useful for the IE practice by decreasing evaluation anxiety, stimulating leadership/staff interest and skills in program evaluation, identifying challenges and opportunities for quality evaluation, improving program evaluability (readiness for evaluation), and increasing evaluation use. That is why a number of authors believe that ECB is part of the line of duty of internal evaluators (Baron, this issue; Love, 1991; Rennekamp & Engle, 2008; Schweigert, this issue; Sonnichsen, 2000; Taylor-Powell & Boyd, 2008; Volkov, 2008). Sonnichsen (2000) stresses the fact that to fulfill the role of the internal evaluator, "the ultimate objective is to build evaluation capacity in the organization to an acceptance level where evaluation is perceived as an indispensable component in the structural, administrative, and operational configuration of the organization" (p. 18). The ECB role of the evaluator translates into enhancing the organization's ability to access, build, and use evaluative knowledge and skills; cultivate a spirit of continuous organizational learning, improvement, and accountability; and create awareness and support for program evaluation and self-evaluation as a performance improvement strategy in the internal and external environments in which it functions (King & Volkov, 2005).

As an example, Rennekamp and Engle (2008) illuminate the work of extension evaluation specialists who successfully build the capacity of local extension educators by serving as consultants, coaches, and trainers. Taylor-Powell and Boyd (2008), describing the ECB role as one of the responsibilities of internal evaluation professionals, note that in a demanding world of organizations, managing the ECB role requires relationship building, stewardship, and vision. The authors also caution us about "a constant challenge to be seen as an ECB practitioner—building skills, processes, and infrastructures—rather than a program evaluator 'doing evaluations,' especially when performing the tasks of program evaluation is the key to securing buy-in and moving individuals and groups into the next level of capacity" (p. 57).

(Management) Decision-Making Supporter

To make a difference in the organization and its programs, the evaluator's role should be integrated in the decision-making process. As stated by Brazil (1999), the functional role of the evaluator includes the one of decision maker, including the principal tasks of analysis, coordination, and policy implementation. Clearly defined as an advisor to program managers, the evaluator is in a better position to influence organizational change.

Being concerned about objectivity of internal evaluation, House (1986) called the internal evaluator an "administrator's tool." The good news, however, is that this management tool is designed to help fix the organization's programs and practices, the belief shared by Brazil (1999), Clifford and Sherman (1983), Kennedy (1983), Love (1983b, 1991), Mathison (1991a), Patton (2008), and Sonnichsen (2000). The internal evaluator's task is to leverage the opportunities to make evaluation of value to the decision makers. Sonnichsen (2000) urges the internal evaluators to switch from a neutral, detached stance to the one of active engagement in the decision-making processes.

Mathison (1991a, p. 162) describes program evaluation as part of overall information-processing activities engaged to monitor and improve the organizational performance and highlights "a necessity for evaluators to operate close to and in the interests of the organization's management" promoted by a decision-making model of evaluation. Patton (2008) also depicts the role of the evaluator as management consultant, decision support, and management information resource. According to Love (1983b), the internal evaluation and planning and management activities have to be interconnected, and the role of evaluator should be as well defined as that of consultant to program managers. Clifford and Sherman (1983) concur that the internal evaluator has a role of a management decision-support specialist in possession of technical, analytical, interpersonal, and organizational skills and the ability to recognize in what situations these management-support skills should be applied to facilitate planning and control functions of managers.

Consultant

The notion of the consultant role is rather wide-ranging. Block (2000) tells us that "[y]ou are consulting any time you are trying to change or improve a situation but have no direct control over the implementation. If you have direct control you are managing, not consulting" (p. xxi). Sounds familiar? That's right, it is about us evaluators. Indeed, according to the same author, "A survey of problems . . . an evaluation, a study—all are consultations for the sake of change. The consultant's objective is to engage in successful actions that result in people or organizations managing themselves differently" (p. 5).

Sonnichsen (2000) promotes "thinking like consultants" (p. 291) and explains that being an evaluator–consultant means the recognition of the fact that formal evaluation is only one of the numerous approaches to problem solving. He goes on by saying that

> Most organizational phenomena are not static and therefore do not easily lend themselves to facile measurement or quantification. However, evaluator–consultants, combining their evaluation expertise, management skills, and institutional memory, can still appropriately examine these phenomena by defining the problem and identifying the correct methodology for addressing the issue. (p. 295)

Clifford and Sherman (1983), Morabito (2002), and Owen and Lambert (1998) emphasize the organizational development consultant role of the evaluator, whereas Love (1983b) and Brazil (1999) perceive the evaluator as an advisor or a consultant to program managers. The primary objective for internal evaluator's consultancy is to generate evaluative processes and information that have a positive effect on the organization and its initiatives. The consultant role requires diverse technical and interpersonal skills, whereas in-depth knowledge of the organization should allow a more effective utilization of consultant skills.

Researcher/Technician

In their daily work, evaluators optimize best practices from the social research field to solve organizational problems. Weiss (1998) believes that the role of a detached, scientific researcher still holds true for the evaluator—in addition to the new, more participative roles. The evaluator is not a basic researcher but rather an "applied researcher," according to Love (2005), and is expected to be engaged in research activities that support organizational development and learning. "Social researcher" and "operations researcher" are those who can handle this kind of work, believe Clifford and Sherman (1983, p. 28).

Skolits et al. (2009) in their overview of the roles driven by evaluation methods cite Noblit and Eaker (1987) to highlight a number of methods-based role orientations, such as positivism (credible expert role), interpretivism (social network broker role), critical theory (emancipator role), aesthetics researcher (connoisseur/critic role), collaborative researcher (broker of interests role), and action research (expert in solidarity with practitioners role). Brazil (1999) explains that a number of organizational situations call for the evaluator's role of a "statistician, where data analysis is the basic task" (p. viii), whereas Mark (2002) introduces the "technical geek" role. Sonnichsen (1988) also writes about a technical role of a policy analyst of topics of importance to top management.

Advocate

Bellavita, Wholey, and Abramson (1986) argue that the contemporary evaluator is a program advocate but "not an advocate in the sense of an ideologue willing to manipulate data and to alter findings to secure next year's funding"; rather, it is "someone who believes in and is interested in helping programs and organizations succeed" (p. 289). Sonnichsen (2000) promotes advocacy evaluation as "an overarching, philosophical, activist orientation that modifies the traditional neutral behavior of internal evaluators by increasing the evaluator's involvement with the organization" (p. 140). To practice advocacy evaluation, the traditional role for internal evaluators should be redefined to include strong interest in and responsibility for the evaluation use. This role overlaps significantly with that of a change agent. As a matter of fact, advocacy evaluation stresses the role of internal evaluators as change agents. Patton (2008) also uses the notions of a champion of evaluation, advocate for intended primary users, and advocate for evaluation use.

Nowadays, as stated by Tarsilla (2010), the question is not about appropriateness of promoting evaluators' values in their practice, but rather about who should be the target of their advocacy. For example, the role of an advocate for the program's target groups is important to Greene (1997). Mertens (2007) also urges evaluators to be concerned about the most vulnerable groups of the program participants in terms of social justice and human rights. I think it is safe to say that Finley Peter Dunne's (1867–1936) "Comfort the afflicted, and afflict the comfortable" principle could be an appropriate credo (or should we say a role?) for program evaluators who would ask pertinent questions, implement proper evaluations, and advocate for their use in introducing positive changes.

Organizational Learning Supporter

Love (2005) believes that one of the important roles of internal evaluation is to support organizational development and learning. Moreover, "the practice of internal evaluation can serve as the basis for organizational learning" (Sonnichsen, 2000, p. 78). This essential role is clearly linked to the roles of the change agent, ECB practitioner, and educator. An evaluator is an educator of the learning processes of evaluative inquiry, according to Preskill and Torres (1999), responsible also for demonstrating them and helping people acquire and practice them. The evaluator should always seek to increase the utility of internal evaluation information for the purpose of advancing organizational learning (Leviton, 2001). The role of contributing to organizational development is also mentioned by Clifford and Sherman (1983), Morabito (2002), and Owen and Lambert (1998).

Internal evaluators guide the organization's staff in the learning process of clarifying goals, questioning their practices, and measuring their outcomes. To be engaged in this process, they need to speak the organization's language, to be in the "organizational know," and to be immersed in the organizational culture by participating in organizational events, committees, work groups, and so on. To be able to facilitate organizational learning, Sonnichsen (2000) also suggests that internal evaluators understand how the organization obtains information and uses it to learn. He calls such practitioners "informed evaluators, with an understanding of the principles of organizational functions, managerial motivations, and information distribution dynamics" (p. 296).

Conclusion

Those who expect to master the world of internal evaluation with nothing more than a goal of conducting program evaluations while assuming that evaluation data and elaborate analytical tools will win the day may find themselves in a great deal of frustration. An emerging phenomenon in the program evaluation field and academic literature is the multiplicity and elasticity of roles of the evaluators, especially those working inside organizations. This chapter addressed various perspectives concerning the internal evaluators in contemporary organizations, offering the reader opportunities to explore "appropriate roles that have the potential to foster an enhanced evaluation process influence" (Morabito, 2002, p. 328).

Figure 3.1 portrays my view, grounded in the literature and my personal experience, of the essential, macrolevel roles that combine to form and affect the composite identity of the modern internal evaluator. The majority of these roles can probably be placed on a continuum's end of so-called role integration described by Ashforth, Kreiner, and Fugate (2000), in other words, the roles with low contrast in role-based identities and flexible and permeable role boundaries.

Figure 3.1. Essential Roles of the Internal Evaluator

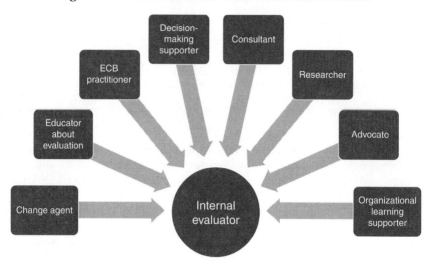

The evaluator's ability to implement these and other roles will be a function of the evaluator's appropriate attitudes, knowledge, and skills, as well as a confluence of enabling contextual factors. Despite the perceived difficulty of the task, many of the roles seem to be within manageable reach, given the evaluator's personal determination and sufficient support provided by the organizational leadership. How we fit and perform in the big picture of all these roles is how we function in general as internal evaluators. The responsibility for determining what roles to assume and when to assume them rests with the evaluator.

New directions for internal evaluation include adaptation, reframing, and harmonization of evaluator roles to fit complex demands of modern organizations. It is my conviction that in fulfilling these harmonized roles the internal evaluator will be able to act as a catalyst for rewiring the brain of an organization by introducing what I would like to call "the evaluation meme" (*meme* is a term that identifies an idea, behavior, or style transmitted from one person or group of people to another within a culture; e.g., see Lynch, 1996). Modern internal evaluators will understand how to integrate evaluation into programs and staff development in a way that reinforces the importance of evaluation, contributes to its habituation, but at the same time prevents its harmful routinization (senseless, repetitive use of the same techniques or instruments). Evaluative thinking is not only a process, but also a mind-set and capacity, in other words, a person's or organization's ability, willingness, and readiness to look at things evaluatively and to strive to utilize the results of such observations. A challenging role for the internal evaluators will be to promulgate such a mind-set throughout the entire organization.

References

Anderson-Draper, M. H. (2006). Understanding cultural competence through the evaluation of "Breaking the silence: A project to generate critical knowledge about family violence within immigrant communities." *The Canadian Journal of Program Evaluation, 21,* 59–79.

Ashforth, B. E., Kreiner, G. E., & Fugate, M. (2000). All in a day's work: Boundaries and micro role transitions. *Academy of Management Review, 25*(3), 472–491.

Barkdoll, G. L. (1982). *Increasing the impact of program evaluation by altering the working relationship between the program manager and the evaluator* (Unpublished doctoral dissertation). University of Southern California, Los Angeles, CA.

Barkley, M. (2001). *Internal evaluation on the edge: Postcards from a postmodern practitioner.* Paper presented at the Australasian Evaluation Society annual conference, "Consolidate, Innovate, Expand," Canberra, Australia.

Bellavita, C., Wholey, J. S., & Abramson, M. A. (1986). Performance-oriented evaluation: Prospects for the future. In J. S. Wholey, M. A. Abramson, & C. Bellavita (Eds.), *Performance and credibility: Developing excellence in public and non-profit organizations.* Lexington, MA: Lexington Press.

Benjamin, L. M., & Greene, J. C. (2009). From program to network: The evaluator's role in today's public problem-solving environment. *American Journal of Evaluation, 30*(3), 296–309.

Block, P. (2000). *Flawless consulting: A guide to getting your expertise used.* San Francisco, CA: Jossey-Bass.

Braverman, M. T., & Arnold, M. E. (2008). An evaluator's balancing act: Making decisions about methodological rigor. *New Directions for Evaluation, 120,* 71–86.

Brazil, K. (1999). A framework for developing evaluation capacity in health care settings. *International Journal of Health Care Assurance, 10,* vi–xi.

Campbell, D. T. (1969). Reforms as experiments. *American Psychologist, 24,* 409–429.

Chelimsky, E. (1994). Making evaluation units effective. In J. S. Wholey, H. P. Hatry, & K. E. Newcomer (Eds.), *Handbook of practical program evaluation* (pp. 493–509). San Francisco, CA: Jossey-Bass.

Chelimsky, E. (2001). What evaluation could do to support foundations: A framework with nine component parts. *American Journal of Evaluation, 22*(1), 13–28.

Christie, C. A. (2008). Interview with Eric Barela. *American Journal of Evaluation, 29*(4), 534–546.

Clifford, D. L., & Sherman, P. (1983). Internal evaluation: Integrating program evaluation and management. *New Directions for Program Evaluation, 20,* 23–45.

Conley-Tyler, M. (2005). A fundamental choice: Internal or external evaluation? *Evaluation Journal of Australasia, 4*(1/2), 3–11.

Cronbach, L. J., & Associates. (1980). *Toward reform of program evaluation: Aims, methods, and institutional arrangements.* San Francisco, CA: Jossey-Bass.

Dahler-Larsen, P. (2006). Evaluation after disenchantment: Five issues shaping the role of evaluation in society. In I. F. Shaw, J. C. Greene, & M. M. Mark (Eds.), *The Sage handbook of evaluation.* London, United Kingdom: Sage.

Dozois, E., Langlois, M., & Blancher-Cohen, N. (2010). *DE 201: A practitioner's guide to developmental evaluation.* Montreal, Canada: The J. W. McConnell Family Foundation.

Duffy, B. P. (1994). Use and abuse of internal evaluation. *New Directions for Program Evaluation, 64,* 25–32.

Everitt, A. (1996). Developing critical evaluation. *Evaluation, 2,* 173–188.

Fitzpatrick, J. L., Sanders, J. R., & Worthen, B. R. (2004). *Program evaluation: Alternative approaches and practical guidelines* (3rd ed.). Boston, MA: Pearson Education.

Fleischer, M. (1983). The evaluator as program consultant. *Evaluation and Program Planning, 6,* 69–76.

Greene, J. C. (1997). Evaluation as advocacy. *Evaluation Practice, 18*(1), 25–36.

Greene, J. C. (2000, November). *Reconsidering roles.* Paper presented at the Annual Meeting of the American Evaluation Association, Honolulu, HI.

Hood, S. (2001). Nobody knows my name: In praise of African American evaluators who were responsive. *New Directions for Evaluation, 92,* 31–43.

Hopson, R. K. (2001). Global and local conversations on culture, diversity, and social justice in evaluation: Issues to consider in a 9/11 era. *American Journal of Evaluation, 22,* 375–380.

Hopson, R. K. (2002). Making (more) room at the evaluation table for ethnography: Contributions to the responsive constructivist generation. In K. E. Ryan & T. A. Schwandt (Eds.), *Exploring evaluator role and identity* (pp. 37–56). Greenwich, CT: Information Age Publishing.

House, E., & Howe, K. (1999). *Values in evaluation and social research.* Thousand Oaks, CA: Sage.

House, E. R. (1986). Internal evaluation. *American Journal of Evaluation, 7*(1), 63–64.

House, E. R. (1993). *Professional evaluation: Social impact and political consequences.* Newbury Park, CA: Sage.

Huberty, C. J. (1982). What/who is an evaluator? In C. J. Huberty & D. A. Payne (Eds.), *Contributions of program and project evaluation* (pp. 3–11). Athens, GA: Educational Research Laboratory.

Huberty, C. (1988). Another perspective on the role of an internal evaluator. *American Journal of Evaluation, 9,* 25–32.

Jenlink, P. M. (1994). Using evaluation to understand the learning architecture of an organization. *Evaluation and Program Planning, 17,* 315–325.

Katz, D., & Kahn, R. (1978). *The social psychology of organizations* (2nd ed.). New York, NY: John Wiley & Sons.

Kennedy, M. M. (1983). The role of the in-house evaluator. *Evaluation Review, 7,* 519–541.

King, J. A., & Stevahn, L. (2002). Three frameworks for considering evaluator role. In K. E. Ryan & T. A. Schwandt (Eds.), *Exploring evaluator role and identity* (pp. 1–16). Greenwich, CT: Information Age Publishing.

King, J. A., & Volkov, B. (2005). A framework for building evaluation capacity based on the experiences of three organizations. *CURA Reporter, 35*(3), 10–16.

Kirkhart, K. E. (2000). Reconceptualizing evaluation use: An integrated theory of influence. *New Directions for Evaluation, 88,* 5–22.

Lambur, M. T. (2008). Organizational structures that support internal program evaluation. *New Directions for Evaluation, 120,* 41–54.

Leviton, L. C. (2001). Presidential address: Building evaluation's collective capacity. *American Journal of Evaluation, 22*(1), 1.

Love, A. J. (1983a). Editor's notes. *New Directions for Program Evaluation, 20,* 1–3.

Love, A. J. (1983b). The organizational context and the development of internal evaluation. *New Directions for Program Evaluation, 20,* 5–22.

Love, A. J. (1991). *Internal evaluation: Building organizations from within.* Thousand Oaks, CA: Sage.

Love, A. J. (2005). Internal evaluation. In S. Mathison (Ed.), *Encyclopedia of evaluation* (pp. 206–207). Thousand Oaks, CA: Sage.

Lyle, C. (2000). Book review of *High impact internal evaluation,* by Richard C. Sonnichsen. *American Journal of Evaluation, 21*(2), 285–288.

Lynch, A. (1996). *Thought contagion. How belief spreads through society. The new science of memes.* New York, NY: Basic Books.

Mark, M. M. (2002). Toward better understanding of alternative evaluator roles. In K. E. Ryan & T. A. Schwandt (Eds.), *Exploring evaluator role and identity* (pp. 17–36). Greenwich, CT: Information Age Publishing.

Mark, M. M., Henry, G. T., & Julnes, G. (2000). *Evaluation: An integrated framework for understanding, guiding, and improving policies and programs.* San Francisco, CA: Jossey-Bass.

Mathison, S. (1991a). What do we know about internal evaluation? *Evaluation and Program Planning, 14,* 159–165.

Mathison, S. (1991b). Role conflicts for internal evaluators. *Evaluation and Program Planning, 14,* 173–179.

Mertens, D. M. (2002). The evaluator's role in the transformative context. In K. E. Ryan & T. A. Schwandt (Eds.), *Exploring evaluator role and identity* (pp. 103–118). Greenwich, CT: Information Age Publishing.

Mertens, D. M. (2007). Transformative considerations: Inclusion and social justice. *American Journal of Evaluation, 28*(1), 86–90.

Minnett, A. M. (1999). Internal evaluation in a self-reflective organization: One non-profit agency's model. *Evaluation and Program Planning, 22*(3), 353–362.

Morabito, S. M. (2002). Evaluator roles and strategies for expanding evaluation process influence. *American Journal of Evaluation, 23,* 321–330.

Newman, D. L., & Brown, R. D. (1996). *Applied ethics for program evaluation.* Thousand Oaks, CA: Sage.

Noblit, G. W., & Eaker, D. J. (1987, April). *Evaluation designs as political strategies.* Paper presented at the Annual Meeting of the American Educational Research Association, Washington, DC.

Owen, J. M., & Lambert, C. L. (1998). Evaluation and the information needs of organizational leaders. *American Journal of Evaluation, 19,* 355–365.

Patton, M. Q. (2008). *Utilization-focused evaluation* (4th ed.). Thousand Oaks, CA: Sage.

Perrin, Burt (2001). Commentary: Making yourself—and evaluation—useful. *American Journal of Evaluation, 22*(2), 252–259.

Preskill, H. (1994). Evaluation's role in enhancing organizational learning: A model for practice. *Evaluation and Program Planning, 17*(3), 291–297.

Preskill, H., & Torres, R. T. (1999). Building capacity for organizational learning through evaluative inquiry. *Evaluation, 5,* 42–60.

Rallis, S., & Rossman, G. (2000). Dialogue for learning: Evaluator as critical friend. *New Directions for Evaluation, 86,* 81–92.

Rennekamp, R. A., & Engle, M. (2008). A case study in organizational change: Evaluation in cooperative extension. *New Directions for Evaluation, 120,* 15–26.

Russ-Eft, D., & Preskill, H. (2001). *Evaluation in organizations: A systematic approach to enhancing learning, performance, and change.* Cambridge, MA: Perseus.

Ryan, K. E., & Schwandt, T. A. (Eds.). (2002). *Exploring evaluator role and identity.* Greenwich, CT: Information Age Publishing.

Sanders, J. R. (2002). Presidential address: On mainstreaming evaluation. *American Journal of Evaluation, 23*(3), 253–259.

Scriven, M. (1991). *Evaluation thesaurus.* Thousand Oaks, CA: Sage.

Scriven, M. (2001). Evaluation: Future tense. *American Journal of Evaluation, 22*(3), 301–307.

Scriven, M. (2007). Activist evaluation. *Journal of Multi-Disciplinary Evaluation, 4*(7), i–ii.

Segerholm, C. (2002). Evaluating as responsibility, conscience, and conviction. In K. E. Ryan & T. A. Schwandt (Eds.), *Exploring evaluator role and identity* (pp. 87–102). Greenwich, CT: Information Age Publishing.

Senge, P. (1997). Comments during satellite discussion of issues in education at the Annual Meeting of the Texas Association for the Supervision of Curriculum Development, Houston, TX.

Shulha, L. M., & Cousins, J. B. (1997). Evaluation use: Theory, research, and practice since 1986. *Evaluation Practice, 18*(3), 195–208.

Skolits, G. J., Morrow, J. A., & Burr, E. M. (2009). Re-conceptualizing evaluator roles. *American Journal of Evaluation, 30*(3), 275–295.

Sonnichsen, R. C. (1988). Advocacy evaluation: A model for internal evaluation offices. *Evaluation and Program Planning, 11,* 141–148.

Sonnichsen, R. C. (2000). *High impact internal evaluation: A practitioner's guide to evaluating and consulting inside organizations.* Thousand Oaks, CA: Sage.

Stake, R. E. (2004). *Standards-based and responsive evaluation.* Thousand Oaks, CA: Sage.

Stufflebeam, D. L. (2003, October). *The CIPP model for evaluation.* Paper presented at the Annual Conference of the Oregon Program Evaluators Network Conference, Portland, OR.

Tarsilla, M. (2010). Being blind in a world of multiple perspectives: The evaluator's dilemma between the hope of becoming a team player and the fear of becoming a critical friend with no friends. *Journal of MultiDisciplinary Evaluation, 6*(13), 200–205.

Taylor-Powell, E., & Boyd, H. H. (2008). Evaluation capacity building in complex organizations. *New Directions for Evaluation, 120,* 55–69.

Themessl-Huber, M., Harrow, A., & Laske, S. (2005). Evaluator roles. In S. Mathison (Ed.), *Encyclopedia of evaluation* (pp. 147–149). Thousand Oaks, CA: Sage.

Torres, R. T. (1991). Improving the quality of internal evaluation: The evaluator as consultant–mediator. *Evaluation and Program Planning, 14,* 189–198.

Volkov, B. (2008). A bumpy journey to evaluation capacity: A case study of evaluation capacity building in a private foundation. *Canadian Journal of Program Evaluation, 23*(3), 175–197.

Volkov, B., & King, J. A. (2007). *A checklist for building organizational evaluation capacity.* The Evaluation Center: Western Michigan University. Retrieved from http://www.wmich.edu/evalctr/checklists/ecb.pdf

Weiss, C. H. (1998). *Evaluation: Methods for studying programs and policies* (2nd ed.). Upper Saddle River, NJ: Prentice-Hall.

Whitmore, E. (1998). Final commentary. *New Directions for Evaluation, 80,* 95–99.

Wholey, J. S. (1983). *Evaluation and effective public management.* Boston: Little, Brown.

Williams, D., & Hawkes, M. (2003). Issues and practices related to mainstreaming evaluation: Where do we flow from here? *New Directions for Evaluation, 99,* 63–85.

BORIS B. VOLKOV *is an assistant professor of evaluation studies with the Center for Rural Health and Department of Family and Community Medicine at the University of North Dakota School of Medicine.*

Schweigert, F. J. (2011). Predicament and promise: The internal evaluator as ethical leader. In B. B. Volkov & M. E. Baron (Eds.), *Internal evaluation in the 21st century. New Directions for Evaluation, 132,* 43–56.

4

Predicament and Promise: The Internal Evaluator as Ethical Leader

Francis J. Schweigert

Abstract

Internal evaluators encounter risks but also significant opportunities to strengthen organizational and professional ethics. Potential contributions depend, in part, on the conjunction of ethics and evaluation in the role of the internal evaluator as the person specially commissioned to investigate value and render judgment based on evidence gathered. At the same time, risks increase when evaluation and ethics are brought together. In the words of one evaluator, "These are rather dangerous moments because a lot of energy is created when an evaluator expresses ethical values such as these. We have a great deal of power, whether we like to think so or not" (Cartland, 2010). This article clarifies the risks in order to free up the potential. © Wiley Periodicals, Inc., and the American Evaluation Association.

E thics is often considered synonymous with morals or values, but distinguishing these concepts can shed light on the unique and powerful relationship between evaluation and ethics. Ethics is distinct from morals and values in much the same way that evaluation is distinct from value, results, and performance: Both ethics and evaluation employ disciplined inquiry to reach reasoned judgment on complex operations under conditions of public scrutiny. For internal evaluators, this conjunction of ethics and evaluation brings risks but also significant opportunities to strengthen organizational and professional ethics. Potential contributions depend, in part, on the role of the internal evaluator as the person specially commissioned to investigate value and render judgment based on evidence gathered. Risks increase when evaluation and ethics are brought together. In the words of one evaluator, "These are rather dangerous moments because a lot of energy is created when an evaluator expresses ethical values such as these. We have a great deal of power, whether we like to think so or not" (Cartland, 2010). This article attempts to clarify the particular risks faced by internal evaluators in order to free up their potential contributions to ethics in evaluation, within organizations, and in the external public arena.

Both ethics and morals function as important mechanisms of social regulation, along with markets, culture and tradition, and law. Each of these five mechanisms contributes to social order in its own way, as well as functioning interdependently with the others. Three of these mechanisms—morals, culture, and markets—appear in all known human societies and are rooted in our evolutionary heritage, so that each individual is born with the experience-expectant genetic equipment to encounter and employ these mechanisms in social life (de Waal, 1996; Iran-Nejad & Marsh, 1993). Ethics and law become important as human societies build on this inherited order, continually converting interactions into patterns of behavior, patterns into expectations, expectations into norms, and norms into institutions (Shapiro, 2011; Wrong, 1994). A brief review of common perceptions of these five regulatory mechanisms can help distinguish the role each plays in building and maintaining social order.

Morality regulates individual and communal interactions through inherited and socialized predispositions but also through conscious individual judgments, that is, individual conscience (de Waal, 1996; Durkheim, 1925/1973; Hauser, 2006). Morality answers questions such as: Is this action right or wrong? Is this circumstance or result good or bad? Are you with us or against us?

Markets regulate the exchange of goods and services, from informal sharing and gifts to formal sales and purchases (Mauss, 1950/1990; Schieffelin, 1990; Schultz, 2001). Markets are governed under an expectation of reciprocity, often worked out in bargaining and negotiation, and frequently finalized in a contract. Markets answer the questions: Is this exchange mutually advantageous? Is this product or service worth the price? Can you be trusted, or not?

Culture and tradition accrue through time as the patterns and tools of behavior that are dependable, useful, comfortable, and meaningful: a shared knowledge often called "common sense" (Lancaster, 1975; Mead, 1930/1975; Whiting & Edwards, 1988). Culture and tradition answer questions such as: Is this food or activity safe? Is this pursuit worthwhile? How important is this relationship? Is this place or behavior sacred?

Laws formalize selected rules and commitments, as these are enacted by legitimate authority (Dworkin, 1986; Shapiro, 2011). According to Scott Shapiro's "planning theory of law," legal systems enable "communities to overcome the complexity, contentiousness, and arbitrariness of communal life by resolving those social problems that cannot be solved, or solved as well, by nonlegal means alone" (2011, p. 171). Law answers such questions as: Are you empowered to decide this matter? How can this activity be coordinated? Is this behavior allowed or mandated?

Ethics in its broadest sense is rational reflection on disputes that arise in the preceding four mechanisms, in which competing claims are weighed and resolved under standards of public reason (Frankena, 1963; Strauss, 1953). Thus, ethics answers the questions: Is this duty or claim binding on all? Is this action or its result just?

Ethics is the regulatory mechanism that enables communities, organizations, associations, or jurisdictions to dispute about right and wrong or worth and value in accord with public reason. It is an exercise aimed at common understanding rather than a matter of personal moral conviction, leading to public recognition or agreement. Even though ethical disputes are not settled once and for all, the attempts nevertheless define a just social order as best it can be understood.

The interdependence of these five mechanisms, and in particular the role of ethics, can be illustrated in reference to markets. Markets generally work well to employ human talent efficiently and distribute goods equitably. In doing so, markets coordinate exchange with a common sense of culture and tradition as well as morals such as honesty of information and concern for the common welfare (Schultz, 2001). Where necessary, societies enact laws to regulate these coordinations (Shapiro, 2011, p. 213), but conflicting moral claims require translating matters of morals into matters of ethics to determine what is just or unjust. As Ronald Dworkin observed, "Justice is a matter of the correct or best theory of moral and political rights [whereas law] is a matter of which supposed rights supply a justification for using or withholding the collective force of the state" (1986, p. 97). For example, the income tax is legal because it has been instituted as law by a body empowered to do so. I may believe the income tax is morally wrong and act on this conviction as a matter of personal moral integrity. To claim the income tax is unjust, however, requires that I state reasons under the standard of public reason and present these for public deliberation. A determination of justice is a matter of reasoned deliberation and judgment, rather than personal moral conviction, market reciprocity, tradition, or a fact of law. Full respect can be given to these other mechanisms, but attempts to obligate the public on the basis of cultural traditions or personal moral convictions are subject to ethical challenge. Ethics therefore functions as regulator of the other social regulatory mechanisms, analogous to the way that evaluation functions as the discipline upon which determinations of quality in other disciplines depends (Scriven, 2011). As John Rawls pointed out,

"Justice is the first virtue of social institutions, as truth is of systems of thought. A theory however elegant and economical must be rejected or revised if it is untrue; likewise, laws and institutions no matter how efficient and well-arranged must be reformed or abolished if they are unjust" (1971, p. 3). Ethics and justice are consequently always open to dispute. New claims of injustice can be brought before the public and old claims can be renewed; ethics and justice are by definition an incomplete enterprise.

The Predicament of the Internal Evaluator

The public's trust in the professions—and its ethical claim on the professions—is based on each profession's adherence to its standards and ideals of practice rather than merely on the satisfaction of particular clients. This ethical commitment was summarized by the sociologist Robert Bellah as the "tripartite structure of professional life" in the relationship between professionals, their clients, and professional standards:

> Lawyers, for example, are certainly obligated to help their clients, but as officers of the court their higher obligation is to the law itself; put in the strongest terms, to justice though the heavens fall. When lawyers fail these higher standards in the unprincipled pursuit of their clients' interests they violate the norms of their profession. Similarly doctors, even though their obligation is to care for their patients, have a higher obligation expressed traditionally in the Hippocratic oath. This higher obligation, though it is to serve the interest of the patient, does not entail necessarily following the patient's wishes. (Bellah, 1997, pp. 33–34)

Similarly, the ethical claim upon evaluation is that it be practiced with fidelity to its own standards of evidence, analysis, and judgment—in addition to and preeminent to serving clients' interests. Nothing can replace this priority of ethical practice as the cornerstone of public trust.

The priority of ethics applies to the work of internal evaluators and externally contracted evaluation alike. As Mathison pointed out, "There seems to be no concrete evidence in the literature to support the contention that the nature of ethical dilemmas differs depending on whether one is an internal or external evaluator" (1999, p. 26). There is, however, an added complication for internal evaluators: dual loyalty. All evaluators owe loyalty to the public in their fidelity to evaluation standards, but internal evaluators also owe loyalty to their organization of hire where they serve as a member of the staff. Familiarity and fellowship as co-workers can also reduce the aura of external expertise (Mathison, 1999, p. 30), further heightening organizational loyalty.

The internal evaluator's ethical challenges have deeper roots than personal sensitivities and loyalties, however, because co-workers in fact constitute a "normative reference group" that shapes moral perceptions and values in the workplace. As investigated by the anthropologist Raoul Naroll, the organizational workplace has taken the place of the traditional village or community as that face-to-face community in which moral norms are personalized and enforced:

> Everyone knows everyone else, watches everyone else, gossips about everyone else. It is [where] the moral ideas of the tribe are transmitted, are transformed through gossip from theory to moral pressure. And it is primarily [where] individuals may gain or lose the esteem or respect of their fellow men and women. (Naroll, 1983, p. 136)

Organizations become the normative reference group for the standards of mutual respect, productive participation on a team, living up to professional expectations, formation of personal identity, and self-esteem in a sense of increasing competence. Mutual protection is earned as members of a team defend one another's reputation, fend off external demands, and guard their collective work. Each individual feels a moral obligation to contribute to the success of the team and organization, and each is held accountable to do so. For most workers, this ongoing moral approval is the surest daily guide to how well one is doing one's job. Conversely, moral disapproval in the workplace is a bitter experience; informal sanctions by co-workers can range from the social isolation of averted eyes and missed invitations to open shaming in front of co-workers or retaliatory reports to superiors.

The internal evaluator participates in this scene of moral interdependence—carefully balanced and navigated as it is—with a professional obligation to meet a standard beyond moral approval: a standard of public trust and accountability. In the same way that justice is not defined by personal moral convictions, the evaluator's judgments of value cannot be determined by workplace approval. Of course, internal evaluators are as sensitive to the dynamics of moral approval and disapproval as any other workers, and their sense of self-worth and self-identity are tied up in organizational membership. Yet even though other workers can often depend upon moral approval or disapproval as their daily guide, the integrity of evaluation practice requires that evaluators step outside the world of moral approval in order to do their job.

The same ethical standard applies if managers interfere with the integrity of evaluation practice, for example, to change or suppress evaluation findings.

If their managers succumb to this temptation, evaluators must act. They may attempt to educate their managers, include a dissent in all reports released, refuse to sign the evaluation, refuse the assignment (raising the ethical issues in appealing any resulting disciplinary action), and/or look for new employment. Reference to a clearly stated and widely accepted code of ethics such as the AEA's Guiding Principles may be very helpful in taking any of these actions (Lovell, 1995, p. 62).

As can happen in any profession, evaluators may respond to these pressures by corrupting their practice. This corruption may be as simple as avoiding evaluation questions that might embarrass the organization or bring to light problems that would be costly to correct. It may require endorsing organizational communications or commitments without pointing out contradictions with the organization's mission or code of ethics. Corruption can appear in evaluation reports that downplay findings that might jeopardize a renewal of funding or receipt of organizational awards. Corruption is sometimes inadvertently encouraged by the promise of incentives such as merit pay or the more subtle but powerful exchange of favors between internal evaluators and program managers, all the way up to the CEO. In all these cases, evaluators may believe they are acting selflessly for the benefit of the organization, without admitting that they may have aligned their own interests with those of their employer and thus sacrificed their profession's integrity and the public's trust.

Here, then, are the unique responsibilities and risks that constitute the internal evaluator's predicament. In the course of performing their service, internal evaluators encounter ethical challenges typical of external evaluators and other professions, but also incur ethical challenges unique to their role in regard to organizational loyalty and the risk of isolation or corruption.

The Promise of the Internal Evaluator: The View From Nowhere

Given the predicament of the internal evaluator, we can at the same time see the power in this role to strengthen the ethics of organizations and evaluation practice. Although the risks inherent in this role can be seen as putting the internal evaluator in a "weak position" to confront organizational injustices or ethical lapses (Mathison, 1999, p. 32), the risks also highlight evaluators' authority to shape the moral order within their organizations. This authorizing power rests upon their professional and assigned responsibility to assess performance and results in light of objective, systematically gathered evidence and reasoned analysis.

The internal evaluator's role is primarily regulative rather than productive (programming and results) or directive (as is management). However invested internal evaluators may be in the success or direction of the organization, they occupy a unique position within the organization as its view from the outside—viewing the organization's work and results with the eye of Adam Smith's "impartial spectator" (Smith, 1790/1984), reflecting back to their co-workers an objective view of their work. Herein lies the promise of the internal evaluator's role: seeing the organization and its performance with the insider's insight and at the same time taking a deliberate stand on objectivity: a "view from nowhere" (Nagel, 1986).

NEW DIRECTIONS FOR EVALUATION • DOI: 10.1002/ev

It is customary to think of evaluation as the systematic investigation of value, in terms of merit, worth, and significance (M. Scriven, personal communication, March 9, 2005). Most obviously, the value in question is in the work of the evaluand, but matters of value pervade the practice of evaluation:

> After all, evaluation is a politicized and judgmental practice, and both politics and judgments inherently involve values. In terms of politics, evaluation is often intended to inform policy, itself a values-laden enterprise. In terms of judgments values are integrally embedded in the selection of evaluation purpose, audience, and priority questions to answer, and especially in the criteria that are used to make judgments of program quality. The major task of evaluation is to render judgments of "goodness," which are anchored in a selected set of criteria that privilege some values over others. (Greene, 2010)

As the impartial spectator, evaluators must ground their judgment not merely in accord with the interests of the evaluand or their own personal moral or methodological preferences, but always with an eye to objective value, that is, value as weighed in the public view and presented and defended in terms of public reason: arguments that are valid and sound, employing objective evidence. This can mean questioning organizational values at every stage of the evaluation: purpose, audience, design, methodology, findings, reporting, and recommendations. It can also put the evaluator in the position of giving voice to the concerns of the larger public in regard to the impact of the work in question. This is not advocacy, but accuracy and objectivity—elucidating value in the enterprise in terms of objective benefit to those intended to be served and improved conditions in which they live.

The elucidation of value is sometimes a matter of making explicit what is subjectively valued by co-workers—an exercise similar to a typical values-clarification exercise. This can present difficulties, however, if objectively gathered data do not conform to organizational values or assumptions. Evaluators can face the objection that they are merely imposing their own personal values over the personal values of others, asserting a privileged professional viewpoint that is merely posing as neutral. To meet this objection, evaluators stand on two social facts: *First*, objectivity is not another subjective view with merely relative significance: your view vs. mine. There are essential elements of objectivity to which evaluators hold their work accountable:

1. a public framework of thought, with judgments and conclusions based on reasons and evidence;
2. the use of norms of correct judgment, such as logical argument and rules of evidence;
3. an order of reasons based on principles and criteria;
4. a viewpoint distinguishable from a particular point of view;

5. an account of agreement upon methods of evidence and argument; and
6. the ability to explain disagreements (Rawls, 1996, pp. 110–112).

Second, evaluators hold strictly to neutrality of aim: not allowing their own comprehensive beliefs or personal point of view to corrupt their evaluation design, conduct, or reporting. Rather, evaluators commit themselves to the procedural values of impartiality, consistency, and equal opportunity, and it is these procedural values that give the evaluator's work its objectivity, authority, and utility (Rawls, 1988, pp. 261–262).

Excellence in evaluation practice requires taking a professional stand apart from—although not necessarily against—self-interest and organizational loyalty. The evaluator identifies with the objective view of the work in question. In countless meetings and consultations within the organization, the evaluator has opportunities to share this impartial view taking with co-workers: how to stand back from the fray of engagement, to examine accumulated evidence, to insist upon accuracy, to ground findings on evidence and judgments on analysis of the findings. This is the evaluative thinking that Patton (2008) explicitly linked to evaluation capacity building:

> Building the evaluation capacity of an organization to support staff in thinking evaluatively means integrating evaluation into the organization's culture. This goes well beyond a focus on using the results of isolated studies. It takes us into the arena of organizational culture, looking at how decision makers and staff incorporate evaluative thinking into everything they do as part of ongoing attention to mission fulfillment and continuous improvement. (p. 157)

Robert Stake described this as shifting from episodic thinking to criterial thinking, from the immediacy and personalization of experience to look at "attributes, properties, traits, characteristics, facets, and dimensions" (Stake, 2004, p. 15). Evaluative thinking can enter into the moral order of the organization and be extended in organizational culture. The potential impact can extend beyond concerns with program performance to objective view taking in personnel performance, self-image, respect for diversity, and organizational impact on the public good.

> In doing so, evaluation creates an ethical space—that is, a space defined by a temporary suspension of moral ethical assumptions. We will assume in this space a vacuum of intentions, a sense of anticipation, that its boundaries are given by abutting edges of varying expectations and perspectives . . . This is a space in which some people are invited to make novel judgements about the work of others, and in which the nature of those novel judgements can be regulated and scrutinized. It is in making relatively transparent the basis of judgement, that is, providing the data which people can interpret in different ways, that we add the ethical dimension. Ethical space invites regulation, the re-imposition of ethical order. . . (Kushner, 2000, p. 150)

The evaluator takes a leading role in building evaluation capacity, not only as one skilled in the methods of research but as one practiced in a way of thinking and acting. The evaluator exemplifies the building of evaluation capacity through fidelity in the practice of evaluation, in the long-standing tradition of ethical character formation through the practice of virtue (Aristotle, trans. 1962; Gadamer, 1976/1981; Lickona, 1991; MacIntyre, 1984).

The Promise of the Internal Evaluator: Public Ethics and Public Deliberation

The focus up to this point has been the promise of the internal evaluator within the workings of the organization of hire. A second dimension of promise lies in the extension of organizational influence through the reporting and use of evaluation findings in the public arena. This external dimension of the internal evaluator's promise appears in two ways: the faithful implementation of policies and programs (the extension of public authority into practice) and the use of evaluation findings to inform program design and policy formation (the extension of practice into programming and policy).

Faithful implementation cannot be blind obedience: compliance with program specifications and policy regulations requires interpretation at every turn, to see what the rule requires in this particular situation and how its meaning can be realized here and now. For every situation that is clear-cut and obvious, there are others in which extenuating circumstances or lack of information make the rule more difficult to apply or in which rules are in conflict with each other. Citing the example of mandated terms of study for a government program, Robert Lovell asked,

> Suppose that the time limitation does not allow for study observations over a sufficient time period, for example, to account for a likely seasonal effect. Since the request is a matter of law, the evaluators' managers may be unable to obtain a time frame adjustment. Should the evaluators refuse the assignment, possibly resulting in an even less-informed decision and creating a possible disciplinary problem? Or should the evaluators complete the evaluation, clearly noting the limitations imposed, even though the product will not meet the "highest appropriate technical standards" envisioned in section IIIA.1 of the American Evaluation Association *Guiding Principles for Evaluators.* (Lovell, 1995, p. 62)

Compliance with laws and rules is first of all an act of understanding that must be repeated as practice and interpretation succeed each other, gradually revealing more meaning in the original intention of the rule. The evaluator plays a key role in this process, *first* by creating "a properly reflective distance" from the work at hand; *second* by enabling program and policy to "organize action, in the sense that they configure it, give it form and sense" (Ricoeur, 1986/1991, p. 195). This occurs early in the evaluation process through clarification of goals and rules and through identification of criteria and indicators; it continues through tracking evidence of implementation and results. The evaluator thus assures that resources will be used in accord with the purposes intended, thus upholding the integrity of policy and planning.

The converse of faithful implementation is the translation of learning from practice into program improvements and policy, as the findings and recommendations of evaluators guide future action. This guidance can appear as lessons learned or—more ambitiously—as best practices, benchmarks, revised standards, or performance mandates. It must be noted that powerful self-interests can skew evaluation findings and recommendations to influence policies, resource allocations, regulations, or product approvals, for example, in pharmaceutical trials (House, 2006). Here the ethical practice of evaluation must stand as the public's guardian of the credibility of evidence-based planning and policy; on this the credibility and authority of evaluation itself depends.

Internal evaluators can also play an important role in assessing and expressing their organization's interactions, achievements, and impact in the public arena. The satisfaction of legal or grantor requirements alone does not always ensure that justice has been served. It lies within the internal evaluator's purview to ask if programs are carried out in a manner that affirms human dignity, human community, and fair terms of cooperation. Similarly, evaluators can examine results achieved for evidence of social benefit and just allocation of goods and services.

New Directions in Public Ethics

The promise and power of the internal evaluator can be summarized in three constructions of justice. These bring into focus, as well, the role of evaluation in addressing a crucial gap that has emerged in public ethics in recent decades.

First, justice is constructed in each person as citizen, each of whom is considered capable of acting in accord with the General Will as well as in his or her own self-interest (Rousseau, 1762/1967). Internal evaluators support this work of justice by building evaluation capacity and nurturing evaluative thinking within their organizations: taking the view from nowhere, to act in accord with the public good. This capacity is strengthened through staff training or workshops, but even more importantly in the process of evaluation itself. Each internal evaluator is a coach in evaluative thinking, helping each member of the staff think as a citizen, objectively, systematically, and fairly in terms of the merit, worth, and significance of implementation and results.

Second, justice is constructed as "the good of another" (Aristotle, trans. 1962). It is not enough to see the internal evaluator as the quality assurance officer to help the organization maximize its own efficiency and service delivery. To embody the determination of value in the organization's work fully, the evaluator's perspective cannot stop at the boundaries of the organization but must look to external effects and credibility as well. *Value cannot be defined solely as value to the organization.* When fellow staff members might feel threatened in taking responsibility for the impact of their work and rather take shelter behind a supervisor, internal evaluators can provide crucial support by asking the tough questions:

> What is your own responsibility for the actions you take when you are carrying out instructions? To what extent should you take the initiative to raise issues with or make recommendations to your superiors? Do you tell political and administrative superiors what they want to hear or provide honest and complete analysis? (Svara, 2007, p. 41)

Third, justice is constructed in the arrangement of basic institutions such as organs of government, human rights, and the fair terms of cooperation in markets and politics (Rawls, 1971). Without the regulation that justice provides, these institutions would be shaped entirely in accord with inherited traditions or the preferences of those with the power to impose their own interests. Because justice is determined through public deliberation under the standards of public reason, the objective evidence provided through evaluation is crucial. To give one of many possible examples, schools may or may not be serving their educative purpose; this determination depends, in part, on evaluation of the quality of their performance. The predominant mood among legislators favors a results-oriented regime of standardized testing to measure quality of instruction, even though evaluators are aware that confounding influences can weaken this causal link:

> Test scores are an inadequate proxy for quality because too many factors outside of the teachers' control can influence student performance from year to year—or even from classroom to classroom during the same year. Often, more than half of those teachers identified as the poorest performers one year will be judged average or above average the next, and the results are almost as bad for teachers with multiple classes during the same year. (Bausell, 2011, p. 12)

Bausell proposed adding a process measure with high correlation to instructional value-added: "measuring the amount of time a teacher spends delivering relevant instruction" (p. 12). This is a good example of the kind of contribution internal evaluators can make in the formulation of governmental or organizational policy and thus in the establishment of justice in the public arena.

Just as ethics is the discipline that enables citizens to consider the public good apart from their own partial benefits, evaluation is the discipline that provides credible evidence and judgments of value to inform them in doing so. This is the fundamental role of evaluation as a social institution, without which it would cease to function as a profession performing a public office and instead become merely a tool for public relations or an expertise for hire.

Recent decades have seen a shift in public culture that highlights evaluation's crucial role in justice, marked in some ways by widespread endorsement of the New Public Management model proposed in *Reinventing Government* (Osborne & Gaebler, 1992). In this model, administrators are expected to take a business approach to government, providing services to citizen–customers in the public marketplace. Administrators are no longer seen as mere implementers, but rather as entrepreneurs and inventors in service delivery; the legislature determines which results are expected and leaves administrators to figure out how to achieve these results. Legislators see their ethical obligations embodied in the outcomes expected rather than in the means employed; administrators, leaving matters of justice to the legislature, can pursue the ends expected in whatever way works best, assuming "the end justifies the means" (and basic rights are respected). Both legislators and administrators entrust ethical accountability more to the working of the marketplace than to regulation: The most efficient and effective means are assumed to guide service delivery to maximum social benefit by the "invisible hand" of market pressures.

This displacement of ethical responsibility from administrators upon legislators and both upon the marketplace does not honor the social facts. As John Rawls remarked long ago, "the market fails altogether in the case of public goods" (Rawls, 1971, p. 272).

For administrators and legislators to take responsibility for justice in public policy formation and implementation requires that they take the objective view embodied in evaluation, holding their implementation and results publicly accountable to evidence of performance and impact on the human condition. In support of this commitment to justice, internal evaluators can provide the crucial support of evaluative thinking—the view from nowhere. This includes, as an ordinary interest of evaluation, the assessment of the ethical implications of programs that are being evaluated, informing not only internal government operations but public deliberations as well. Internal evaluators can support public deliberation on matters of justice by setting forth the objective basis for claims. What, in fact, are the responsibilities and commitments of office? What are the conditions and requirements of public participation, and how well do these satisfy the requirements of procedural fairness and human dignity? How are goods and services being allocated, and can this distribution be justified in reasonable terms of merit or need? These questions can be investigated, and where their agencies are involved, it lies within the duties of internal evaluators to investigate them.

References

Aristotle. (1962). *Nicomachean ethics* (M. Ostwald, Trans.). Englewood Cliffs, NJ: Prentice Hall. (Original circulated ca. 335–323 B.C.E.)

Bausell, R. B. (2011, May 1). A new measure for classroom quality. *The New York Times*, p. 12.

Bellah, R. N. (1997). Professions under siege: Can ethical autonomy survive? *Logos, 1*(3), 31–50.

Cartland, J. (2010, December 13). Re: Thought Leaders Forum: RE: Jennifer Greene AEA thought leader. Retrieved from: the American Evaluation Association Discussions: http://comm.eval.org/EVAL/EVAL/Discussions/ViewThread/Default.aspx?GroupId=91&UserKey=099d2c88–67f9–4806–981a–9a8efec27741&MID=809

de Waal, F. (1996). *Good natured: The origins of right and wrong in humans and other animals.* Cambridge, MA: Harvard University Press.

Durkheim, E. (1973). *Moral education: A study in the theory and application of the sociology of education* (E. K. Wilson & H. Schnurer, Trans.). New York, NY: The Free Press. (Original work published 1925)

Dworkin, R. (1986). *Law's empire.* Cambridge, MA: Harvard University Press.

Frankena, W. K. (1963). *Ethics.* Englewood Cliffs, NJ: Prentice-Hall.

Gadamer, H. G. (1981). What is practice? The conditions of social reason. In F. G. Lawrence (Trans.), *Reason in the age of science* (pp. 69–87). Cambridge, MA: The MIT Press. (Original work published 1976).

Greene, J. C. (2010, December 12). Re: Thought Leaders Forum: RE: Jennifer Greene AEA thought leader. Retrieved from: http://comm.eval.org/EVAL/EVAL/Discussions/ViewThread/Default.aspx?GroupId=91&UserKey=099d2c88–67f9–4806–981a–9a8efec27741&MID=809

Hauser, M. D. (2006). *Moral minds: How nature designed our universal sense of right and wrong.* New York, NY: Ecco/HarperCollins Publishers.

House, E. R. (2006, October 28). Blowback: Consequences of evaluation for evaluation. *American Journal of Evaluation, 29*(4), 416–426. doi: 10.1177/1098214008322640

Iran-Nejad, A., & Marsh G. E., III. (1993). Discovering the future of education. *Education, 114,* 249–257.

Kushner, S. (2000). *Personalizing evaluation.* Thousand Oaks, CA: Sage.

Lancaster, J. B. (1975). *Primate behavior and the emergence of human culture.* New York, NY: Holt, Rinehart and Winston.

Lickona, T. (1991). *Educating for character: How our schools can teach respect and responsibility.* New York, NY: Bantam Books.

Lovell, R. G. (1995). Ethics and internal evaluators. *New Directions for Program Evaluation, 66,* 61–67.

MacIntyre, A. (1984). *After virtue: A study in moral theory* (2nd ed.). Notre Dame, IN: University of Notre Dame Press.

Mathison, S. (1999, Summer). Rights, responsibilities, and duties: A comparison of ethics for internal and external evaluators. *New Directions for Evaluation, 82,* 25–34.

Mauss, M. (1990). *The gift: The form and reason of exchange in archaic societies* (W. D. Walls, Trans.). New York, NY: W. W. Norton. (Original work published 1950)

Mead, M. (1975). *Growing up in New Guinea.* New York, NY: William Morrow and Company. (Original work published 1930, 1958, 1962)

Nagel, T. (1986). *The view from nowhere.* New York, NY: Oxford University Press.

Naroll, R. (1983). *The moral order: An introduction to the human situation.* Beverly Hills, CA: Sage.

Osborne, D., & Gaebler, T. (1992). *Reinventing government: How the entrepreneurial spirit is transforming the public sector.* Reading, MA: Addison-Wesley.

Patton, M. Q. (2008). *Utilization-focused evaluation* (4th ed.). Thousand Oaks, CA: Sage.

Rawls, J. (1971). *A theory of justice.* Cambridge, MA: Harvard University Press.

Rawls, J. (1988). The priority of right and ideas of the good. *Philosophy and Public Affairs,* *17,* 251–276.

Rawls, J. (1996). *Political liberalism.* New York, NY: Columbia University Press.

Ricoeur, P. (1991). *From text to action: Essays in hermeneutics, II* (K. Blamey & J. B. Thompson, Trans.). Evanston, IL: Northwestern University Press. (Original work published 1986)

Rousseau, J. J. (1967). *The social contract* (H. J. Tozer, Trans.). In L. G. Crocker (Ed.), *The social contract and discourse on the origin of inequality* (pp. 1–147). New York, NY: Washington Square Press. (Original work published 1762)

Schieffelin, B. B. (1990). *The give and take of everyday life.* New York, NY: Cambridge University Press.

Schultz, W. J. (2001). *The moral conditions of economic efficiency.* New York, NY: Cambridge University Press.

Scriven, M. (2011, January 9). Thought Leaders Forum, RE: Michael Scriven, one who needs very little introduction. Retrieved from: American Evaluation Association Discussions: http://comm.eval.org/EVAL/EVAL/Discussions/Message/Default.aspx?MID=817

Shapiro, S. J. (2011). *Legality.* Cambridge, MA: Harvard University Press.

Smith, A. (1984). *The theory of moral sentiments* (D. D. Raphael & A. L. MacFie, Eds.; 6th ed.). Indianapolis, IN: Liberty Fund. (Original work published 1790)

Stake, R. E. (2004). *Standards-based and responsive evaluation.* Thousand Oaks, CA: Sage.

Strauss, L. (1953). *Natural right and history.* Chicago, IL: University of Chicago Press.

Svara, J. H. (2007). *The ethics primer for public administrators in government and nonprofit organizations.* Sudbury, MA: Jones and Bartlett.

Whiting, B. B., & Edwards, C. P. (1988). *Children of different worlds: The formation of social behavior.* Cambridge, MA: Harvard University Press.

Wrong, D. H. (1994). *The problem of order: What unites and divides society.* Cambridge, MA: Harvard University Press.

FRANCIS J. SCHWEIGERT is associate professor and director of the master of public and nonprofit administration program in the College of Management at Metropolitan State University whose research focuses on nonprofit management, public ethics, restorative justice, and evaluation.

Kniker, T. (2011). Evaluation survivor: How to outwit, outplay, and outlast as an internal government evaluator. In B. B. Volkov & M. E. Baron (Eds.), *Internal evaluation in the 21st century. New Directions for Evaluation, 132,* 57–72.

5

Evaluation Survivor: How to Outwit, Outplay, and Outlast as an Internal Government Evaluator

Ted Kniker

Abstract

This chapter describes the author's experience and insights as the chief of evaluation for public diplomacy at the U.S. Department of State, and as a consultant assisting federal agencies in a multitude of evaluation activities relating what helps and hinders internal evaluation functions. The article discusses the challenges faced by the internal evaluators, how they overcame these challenges, and how they compare to trends observed by the author in other federal evaluation offices. Ideas are provided for how to better incorporate evaluation functions into organizational management. © Wiley Periodicals, Inc., and the American Evaluation Association.

> Ted, your job is to quantify the impact of international exchange programs on world peace.
>
> —My supervisor

So began my first few minutes on my first day as an internal government evaluator in the Bureau of Educational and Cultural Affairs (ECA) (U.S. Department of State, 2011) at the United States Information Agency (USIA). This statement from February 1, 1998, encapsulated the assumptions held by managers, peers, stakeholders, and customers about evaluation and challenges that I have encountered, observed, and discussed with colleagues as an evaluator, consultant, and federal employee over the last decade. These faulty notions, several of which are extensions of the unsuccessful roles of internal evaluators articulated by Love (1991), are that evaluations, when managed internally, are

> The exclusive responsibility of the evaluator, like Love's organizational conscience role. In the federal government, we are usually organized functionally with specific duties and assignments, compartmentalized into silos of business excellence that rarely collaborate or share in responsibility and accountability. It is up to the internal evaluator to manage the accountability.

> An administrative task. It is taken for granted, or even ignored, as a support job in the organization, carrying with it a level of respect equal to or less-than-equal to that of human resources (HR), information technology (IT), procurement, or other similar activities, but without the understanding that it is an essential management function.

> A bean-counting or compliance exercise, like Love's number cruncher. Government programs like anecdotes of achievement, and there is strong resistance to reducing program impact to "a number." Success stories abound, but managers often have difficulty giving context to the scope and range of these accounts, or showing that these weren't cherry picked to make the program look good. Yet, there is also an expectation that evaluators can magically quantify the unquantifiable.

> An irrefutable case of evidence for causation. Government workers are strongly mission driven, and have a nearly unshakeable faith their program contributes significantly to the ultimate, long-term public benefit. They often don't understand why it is not easy for professional evaluators to prove beyond a reasonable doubt that their intervention made a positive difference and that the evaluation can be used to justify increased funding. There is little interest in diagnosing programs for improvement, because this might reflect upon administration of the program, or program design, which in turn could cause the program to be eliminated. And if evaluators cannot come up with the evidence they are either incompetent, or the spy/hatchet man (Love, 1991) to cut the program.

> A one-time event. Once we have answered the causation question there is no need to expend more resources on additional evaluation.

I felt like a contestant on the television show *Survivor.* I was stranded on a remote island (government evaluation), with a few tools with which to survive (limited funds and two staff), and only the resourcefulness of my team to address the challenges we would face. I was now part of the management tribe, hoping not to be voted off the island by my team or by my former tribe, the program leaders. I knew I would be competing for survival (budget, staff, and office space) with the other administrative functions in our bureau, and would need to win the variety of challenges put in front of us. These challenges would test our endurance, strength, agility, problem-solving, teamwork, and willpower. Some of these challenges would return rewards—items that allowed the time on the island to be easier—or immunity—the ability to evaluate another day.

A Brief History of Evaluation in the Bureau of Educational and Cultural Affairs

As the new chief of evaluation, I wanted to familiarize myself with previous efforts, so I reviewed the files to identify best practices and avoid recreating the wheel. No documented literature about ECA evaluation existed, only internal reports from the 1980s when evaluation was limited to a handful of program reviews, generally conducted by academics or independent for-eign-affairs specialists. These studies were commissioned on an as-needed, or as-interested, basis by the front office, where typically one senior man-ager oversaw evaluation as one of several duties (Wolloch & Siegel, 1998). The program reviews were almost exclusively qualitative case studies. Although the reviews discussed some program outcomes, the focus of these studies was primarily an assessment of whether the program was working as intended. From my review, it seemed that the audience for these reviews was limited primarily to the bureau's senior leadership. One issue that immediately emerged was lack of organizational ownership of the findings. This seemed to support Winberg's contention that having management as a client is not enough, evaluations need to be marketed (Winberg, 1991, p. 168). It was not evident that the evaluation reports were widely distrib-uted or discussed, and so there was little programmatic investment into fol-lowing up from the evaluations. Based on the number and scope of the reports that existed, one could draw the conclusion that evaluation was not considered essential to the bureau's operations.

In the 1990s there were three efforts to establish an internal evaluation office, each with different approaches and underlying focus. The first two I considered failures because each attempt was radically altered, whereas the last became the foundation for the ongoing evaluation function in ECA and Public Diplomacy. As more pressure surrounding budget justifications was emerging, the leadership in ECA acknowledged that something was needed to provide data on how programs were working so that improved resource allocations could be made. In 1990, the ECA Executive Office used the Pres-idential Management Intern (PMI) program (U.S. Office of Personnel Man-agement, 2011) to hire three recent graduate students at the GS-9 level as internal evaluators to create the first evaluation office. Within approximately a year this effort folded, despite the intellect and skills of the three PMIs, primar-ily because the effort didn't take into account critical human and management factors in a bureaucratic organization. First, the three PMIs were not trained or experienced evaluators; all came from a public administration background with general research-methodology training. This led long-time managers to question their credibility as evaluators, often wondering whether the evaluations were objective studies or directed hatchet jobs sponsored by the budget office to cut programs, again echoing Love's unsuccessful evaluator roles. Second, the three PMIs had relatively little organizational or government experience, a critical condition noted by Sonnichsen (2000), and the most common criticism of their work by my peers was that they could not understand the nuances of the programs or the context in which the programs operated. Third, the evaluation office was placed under the direction of the financial office. Initially, this was a savvy move because a new function needed a patron and the executive officer controlled the resources. However, the downside was that there was little capacity for effective oversight, and combined with the inexperience of the new staff and the executive leaders in evaluation, the function floundered. Fourth, management gave the three PMIs a relatively large, highly visible program to assess. The initial thinking was to establish the office with an evaluation of an important program whose sustainability was questionable. The result was a model easy to condemn because there was too much resistance to the evaluation by the program office and mistakes made in design, methodology selection, data collection, and analysis were made public. Fifth, the arrangement did not take into account the PMIs' expectations. All had been hired under the impression that they would have a typical PMI experience with job rotations to a variety of offices to gain management and leadership skills. Instead, they became frustrated with staying in a single office with a limited focus, all without the ability to get the methodological training they needed. Eventually, the PMIs were allowed to move out of the office and pursue a normal developmental experience. The evaluation function was moved to the Office of Policy and Planning and staffed with a combination of experienced ECA civil servants and Foreign Service officers.

The revamped office began strong in 1992 by recruiting a well-respected, veteran program manager as its chief. The title of Chief, with the GS-14 grade level, lent more authority to the new office. The revised chain of command had the Chief report to the Director of Policy, who reported to the Associate Director, the top ECA position, creating a closer connection to the Bureau's authority structure. This structure is aligned with one of Sonnichsen's 12 factors for high-impact internal evaluation, the evaluation office reporting to a top official in the organization (Sonnichsen, 2000). Initially, the office hired three staff, at GS-12 and -13 levels (Foreign Service Officer 2)—the top of the nonsupervisory professional career path, putting them at an equal level to most program officers and first-line supervisors. As with the first effort, none of the staff had evaluation training or experience. The office added the mandate to build internal evaluation capacity, which was managed by allotting a limited set of funds for "travel grants" to be given to program officers to conduct site visits and compile an evaluation report to be shared with the Bureau's senior leadership. To receive a travel grant, program officers were required to write proposals and be accepted for the funding. Another change was that each evaluator managed a separate project, instead of working collectively on one project, so more projects could be completed. The focus of the evaluations was on the extent of compliance to public descriptions and which programs "worked," although the performance criteria weren't always well defined in the studies. The underlying assumption was that these data would help improve the programs or provide management data for program reduction and realignment, but it prompted many program managers to believe the new evaluation office was a "gotcha function," reminiscent of Love's spy role (Love, 1991), more interested in investigating what was wrong, with a touch of blame and shame, than in identifying improvement opportunities. A major faux pas of the office, in my opinion, was that it saw itself as too independent and implemented a process where the program managers had little input into the design and conduct of the evaluation studies. I observed several instances where the lack of program input resulted in reports submitted to the Associate Director with programmatic inaccuracies and poorly constructed comparisons, leading program managers to spend time writing up defenses to the reports. It created an us-versus-them culture and strong resistance to the evaluation function. Eventually, the office was dismantled in 1995–1996 in efforts to downsize the Bureau.

Then in 1997 a new Deputy Associate Director identified evaluation and performance measurement as a critical management function and decided to reestablish the evaluation office, resourcing it with a small budget for evaluation studies. He commissioned the office to obtain outcome information about programs that fed the strategic planning for the organization. Within 6 years, the internal evaluation office led the agency to achieve the two highest international affairs scores on the Office of Management and Budget Program Assessment Rating Tool (PART), was deemed a "best practice" by the State Department Office of Inspector General, was benchmarked by other government and nonprofit evaluation functions, and was recommended to be a model for other U.S. government evaluation units by OMB. How did this occur?

The Challenge and the Change

When I assumed the duties of chief of evaluation, there were six overarching challenges facing the office—three were conceptual and three operational—that my team focused on to address the charge my supervisor had presented. The first and most immediate challenge was the lack of clearly defined, measurable program goals. Programs had been established legislatively to serve audiences, such as youth, to promote a specific activity, such as a university-to-university partnership, or to address certain thematic areas,

NEW DIRECTIONS FOR EVALUATION • DOI: 10.1002/ev

such as civil society; however, at the time, defining these programs in terms of reducing a particular problem or increasing a benefit based on baseline data was not occurring. None of the 90-plus ECA programs had a documented theory of action. From interviewing program administrators, we learned that most managers had goals defined for the programs, but these were not codified. As part of our evaluation process, we developed goal-oriented program descriptions and logic models for the program offices. This was the first time that many managers had seen a representation of their program linking their activities to the short-term goals of the program and ultimately the longer-term goals of the bureau and its legislative mandate. The results of using the logic models and detailing the operational goals allowed ECA to articulate its public benefit in a more direct way. It also led to goal-oriented requests for proposals (RFPs) which assisted partner organizations craft more targeted, results-oriented programming. Previously, RFPs had been activity oriented—focusing on how well each bidder could conduct an orientation session, for example. The reward for our office was in that we became a trusted resource and advisor, allowing us more access within the organization, instead of being something to fear or ignore.

The second challenge was solving how to evaluate and measure the achievement of mutual understanding. Because there is no mutual understanding index or other standard to compare to, we needed to establish what constituted success in mutual understanding. We asked, "if mutual understanding occurs, how would we know? What would be the indicators of success?" From this perspective we defined three results: (a) change in participants' knowledge of the host country, such as more accurate cultural understandings; (b) change in participants' behavior based upon the acquisition of the new knowledge; and (c) sustained relationships between participants and those they met in the host country, which was a goal stated in the Bureau's authorizing legislation. This conceptualization allowed us to develop a common theory of change for all ECA programs, linking them together, as well as providing a structure around which to build a performance framework. It also helped change the culture within the organization from being narrowly focused on program delivery to understanding that outcomes happen after people return home and that we needed to expand our view of the partici-pant and project life cycle to address support and engagement after U.S. government funds were expended.

Our third challenge was to develop outcome measures for exchange programs. Over the years, exchange programs positioned themselves as winning hearts and minds, and so there was a lot of resistance to trying to quantify "good will." We did not want to abandon the anecdotal information, because much of it powerfully described life-transforming results. But we also had to have more quantifiable data to present to stakeholders. To come up with the measures, we researched a wide variety of program activities, including student assessment and achievement, international development, public affairs and communications, psychological operations, human intelligence, cross-cultural readiness and sensitivity, and democracy and governance. We adapted Kirkpatrick's framework with four levels of training outcomes (Kirkpatrick & Kirkpatrick, 2006), because it meshed nicely with our three areas of results, it was easy to understand and explain, and with outcomes for reaction (satisfaction) and learning that could be measured immediately postprogram, we were able to overcome the myth held by program managers that the results of exchanges happen in the long term and so were immeasurable. By developing measures based only on the four Kirkpatrick levels and linking those to the ECA-level logic model, we were able to give stakeholders numbers around important results and demonstrate how we knew that exchanging individuals could lead to improved relationships between the United States and other countries.

Despite opposing schools of thought about whether performance measurement and evaluation could peacefully coexist in the same function, we deliberately integrated them. We incorporated 10 required questions that covered our key performance indicators into each evaluation project. From this approach we were able to verify the performance data we were collecting efficiently and eventually use the performance data to shape and focus the evaluations. In 2002, we hired an evaluator who also was a performance-measurement specialist to help us refine our approaches in both areas. For us, this was an immunity challenge: by successfully developing a framework that provided credible quantitative information, based upon an accepted model, combined with the qualitative results information already supported by managers, senior managers delegated more authority to us in conducting evaluation and began to talk about evaluation as an essential component of ECA, manifesting another of Sonnichsen's 12 factors, evaluation as a routine organizational function, accepted by the organization's employees and managers (Sonnichsen, 2000). Eventually, we gained a high-level support to develop our own online performance measurement and evaluation tool, which automated our survey and reporting work, became the data warehouse we could use to run more rigorous statistical analyses, and provided more immediate, timely data back to program managers.

The fourth challenge we faced was poor, or nonexistent, data. Because ECA programs were people-oriented programs, and our office was tasked with documenting the outcomes of these programs, contacting former participants was essential. We discovered there was not a central repository for alumni, and if information existed, it was kept by either the U.S. Embassies or by private, partner organizations. Much of the information was not up to date, except for American participants, who constituted about one-fourth of all alumni. We allocated about a third of evaluation project budgets into finding people and updating contact information. This was particularly tricky when working overseas outside of Europe, where telephone books or other easily accessible public databases were not easy to locate or did not exist. A major recommendation from the first collection of evaluations was that ECA needed to invest in tracking and engaging program alumni (Office of Policy and Evaluation, ECA, 2011). Not only was this needed for evaluation, but we could enhance outcomes through the expanded view of participant life cycle by providing support and additional follow-on activities. ECA eventually created an alumni affairs office, which has become a model for other U.S. government–sponsored exchange programs.

The fifth challenge was methodological. As with most evaluations, we struggled with issues around the purity of methodology and rigor versus feasibility within resources and environment. For example, we questioned how we could draw conclusions about programs that operate in 120 countries when we could only collect data in 5 or 6. Most of our programs drew participants through merit-based selection, and so we could not use randomized controlled trials as an experimental design, and had limited funds to conduct quasiexperimental designs. Appropriate comparison groups were difficult to construct within our target audiences, because of self-selection issues. We faced issues with questionnaire or interview delivery. In many countries, alumni were located outside of major cities, did not have reliable mail or Internet systems, and it was cost-prohibitive to send evaluators to them. One of our innovations was to pay for these people to come to the capital cities for focus groups and structured individual interviews. Following the formal data gathering, the embassy would host receptions for the groups, which accomplished two ultimate goals for the Bureau. First, it helped reconnect the embassy staff with alumni, and second, it allowed for informal data gathering. We often obtained more accurate and useful information in the informal settings, due in part to cultural norms of discussing personal accomplishments either in public or within group settings. For example, in one country, one respondent didn't want to share her accomplishments attributable to the program because she didn't want to be perceived as bragging; in another country, we conducted focus groups in which the intended respondent deferred the answer to every question we asked to the senior colleague in the room. We also had to contend with survey issues of length, language, and cultural understanding. Ultimately, we had to tailor each evaluation project to the particular program, set of countries visited, and respondent demographics. It often would take several months and negotiation with embassies to design the evaluations with all of the environmental factors taken into account. To ensure that designs and methodologies were sound and defensible, we included research specialists from other parts of the agency on the review team to comment on the validity and appropriateness of the approaches proposed by the external evaluators. This collaborative networking kept us informed on research issues others were contending with overseas, as well as providing credible peer review.

The sixth challenge, and probably the most critical to success, was organizational and cultural. This involved overcoming the resistance to evaluation held within the bureau. First, we had to change the perception held by managers of what evaluation is. Most indicated to us that evaluation was the tool used to eliminate or reduce programs, publicize all the program's weaknesses, or at worst, subject a manager to public humiliation. Understanding, as we did, that language is a foundational element in mutual understanding, we purposefully changed the language around evaluation. We talked about documenting outcomes and providing information to program managers that they did not have the resources to collect themselves. We engaged the program managers as customers of evaluation instead of hostages. This did not negate our duty of providing strategic information to the bureau leadership, but we began to include multiple customer dimensions in the focus of our efforts. Another tactic we used to build trust was to embed ourselves into the bureau's program offices. Prior to our efforts, the evaluation function was perceived as aloof and exclusive. We wanted to demonstrate a more collaborative, partnership-oriented relationship, so the three staff members acted as account representatives to the three major program elements, which involved participating in staff meetings and proactively meeting the managers and staff. The approach allowed us to remain current about program happenings, provide policy information to the program offices more directly, and most importantly, weigh in on program planning with data and ideas based upon evaluation findings. We also created evaluation steering teams including the program offices to design the evaluations, and solicit input at critical points in the evaluation process so that they had ownership of the projects and their results. We included the program offices in developing a bureau-wide, 3-year evaluation schedule, which fostered discussion at multiple levels on the critical, strategic information they needed, and allowed us to plan for appropriate resources and foster buy-in to our process and priorities. This kind of collaborative, inclusive approach is well documented by Sonnichsen (2000), Emison (2007), and the Government Accounting Office (GAO) (2003), as a component of successful internal evaluation.

Having been on the receiving end of a couple of poorly executed evaluations, I was determined not to repeat the mistakes of the past and had 95% of the evaluations conducted by independent, external third parties. This helped us overcome the perception that evaluation was being used to cut programs for political reasons. It also afforded more training for our evaluation staff as we built into our contracts requirements for staff to serve as one of the evaluation team members and be thoroughly involved in the design and data collection for each project. The arrangement also gave the evaluators a new role—translator between the external evaluators and program managers. We found this to be a critical element of communication, as often these two groups of professionals can talk past one another. We were able to help the external evaluators understand the programs better and help the program offices understand evaluation and the findings better. The arm's-length distance also kept our evaluations credible with OMB and the Hill. Structuring the role of internal evaluator as a project manager also afforded us the capacity to sponsor more evaluation projects. Our staff of four was able to produce nearly 30 evaluations within the first 4 years.

Effective communication internally and externally was another important element in our survival. Internally, we used change-management techniques for building the reputation of our office as well as for each project. Branding and marketing (Winberg, 1991) our office and products was another tactic, which included providing evaluation information in multiple formats for different audiences with specific looks that incorporated elements of marketing design. We knew that many of the consumers of our evaluations would not wade through a 100–200-page report or detailed descriptions of methodology (those are the types of reports we had seen become credenza-ware), so we gave the full reports only to a small number of the program managers and provided copies to anyone interested. We created stand-alone executive summaries, usually between 4 and 10 pages for each project, that were distributed to most stakeholders and partners. We developed one-page summaries using a specific color combination that were easy to spot on a desk filled with papers, which was provided for VIP stakeholders, such as departmental leadership, members of Congress, their staffs, and OMB budget examiners. We crafted a detailed distribution strategy for these products, identifying who would receive what product from which agency official by what medium (hard copy, Web, etc.). With the substantial volume of reports and the targeted communications plan, we were able to provide information about our programs to key internal and external stakeholders on a regular basis.

I often get asked to comment on whether evaluation policies are essential for internal evaluation. I've seen successful and unsuccessful evaluation both with and without policies. Personally, I believe a documented evaluation policy can be helpful, but for me, the vital idea is what is addressed within the policy. Our initial policy covered several organizational conditions described by Sonnichsen, including operating as an independent entity, the authority to self-initiate evaluations, results being incorporated and disseminated throughout the entire organization, and requests for evaluations being received from top officials (Sonnichsen, 2000). The most important element of the initial policy we developed in ECA regarded our final authority over the evaluations, and the only corrections allowed in evaluation reports were for accuracy of facts. The policy provided protection from the pressures of program managers and political appointees. Secondarily, the policy addressed transparency, conveying that all evaluations were for public disclosure, unless previously agreed before a contract was let, or unless it was an internal management review. A third policy component that was crucial in our particular situation was the description of the types of evaluations we were mandated to conduct. The delineation made it clear that we were evaluators and not auditors, and that our focus was on the strategic level, not the operational. Although operational data always emerged within our work, the strategic-outcome focus helped make evaluation "safe" internally and kept us from being used by higher-level department authorities for studies that were to serve limited agendas. A fourth component of the policy dealt with the role of our office as a centralized evaluation function versus the role of the program offices and their management oversight. If the evaluative questions were to obtain outcome and goal oriented information, the evaluation projects were our domain. Program offices were responsible primarily for ensuring compliance reviews and process improvement reviews. Our office handled needs assessments and outcome/impact assessments. Admittedly, from my experience, I'm a fan of centralized evaluation functions, but if roles and responsibilities are well defined, from an organizational learning standpoint, a combination of centralized and decentralized can work well.

The Conquest

The transformation from being dismantled to being heralded a best-practice and model organization was in large part a result of focusing in a systematic way to become a high-performing organization, relentless customer relationship management, and the resolution of the challenges discussed above. High-performing organizations have several characteristics in common, and we tried to emulate these as much as possible (Brache, 2002; National Institute of Standards and Technology, 2011; Performance Breakthroughs, Inc., 2011). The first is a customer-oriented vision, mission, and guiding principles (Federal Quality Institute, 1994). Instead of seeing ourselves as another administrative function, we emulated the mind-set of professional service firms, going so far as to test the waters on becoming service-for-fee oriented. The customer-focused approach mirrors the points made by Sonnichsen (2000), Love (1991) (management consultant as a successful role), and Emison (2007). Second, high-performing organizations assess their progress toward the vision and mission and develop competencies in three key areas (Federal Quality Institute, 1994; National Institute of Standards and Technology, 2011): (a) our people—what were we doing to demonstrate effective leadership within the bureau, within the department, and within the evaluation field; and how were we ensuring the team was properly trained and committed to the work; (b) our systems—was our planning getting us to where we wanted to go; were we measuring the right things for our own performance; how were we improving our processes and making them more efficient; and (c) our contributions—we became part of the bureau's planning team and were able to incorporate performance measurement and evaluation reviews into the planning process. We also focused on our abilities to respond to stakeholder requests, adopting the attitude that if a stakeholder reached out to us, even if we weren't the appropriate office, we still owned the issue. We worked extremely hard to develop and maintain positive relationships with OMB in particular. Through managing the communication and interaction, we gained a much better understanding of the Program Assessment Rating Tool (PART) and what would satisfy the examiner in our responses, and we were better able to communicate our results, which resulted in the bureau's programs receiving a 97 and 98 on the PART

(Office of Management and Budget, 2008), the highest ratings in the international affairs area. Additionally, the relationship management worked to secure a generic OMB approval for all of our evaluation and data-collection work. Third, we had a strong feedback and learning cycle for our work. We ensured that we built in briefings when evaluations concluded and worked with the program offices to provide them guidance on how to read evaluation reports and discuss and follow up on the findings and recommendations.

The Conclusions

The evolution of ECA evaluation highlights what I personally have found to be the following common set of constraints for government evaluation in general.

Lack of Will

This lack of interest or support by senior management and the organization for internal evaluation, noted by Sonnichsen (2000) as an evaluation obstacle, in my experience is often attributable to an inability to define a persuasive value proposition for evaluation. The key to overcoming this constraint is to recognize that consumers of evaluation are customers, and that in today's world it is customer service and support that distinguish the great from the good. We recognized that there were multiple customers for any evaluation report, all of whom had different information needs, and our job was to balance the needs with the methodologies and the resources. In a sense, we had to segment our customers and deliver the features and benefits of evaluation to them in ways that resonated with them specifically. For example, in one evaluation our Assistant Secretary at the time had heard of problems in a particular program and he wanted those explored; the U.S. Embassies needed information that would help recruitment for the program, specifically the benefits that participants reported from the program; the program office wanted information from a longitudinal perspective to be able to identify trends and correlate those with changes in policies over time; and OMB wanted data on results in relationship to costs invested. We were able to meet all of these objectives. Most importantly, though, we found that the more data were shared with these customers and stakeholders, the more they came to rely and depend upon it, gradually making us an invaluable resource. Whereas when I started with evaluation people were wary of it, within 4 years we had program managers asking to have their programs evaluated by us, and were willing to contribute their own program money. They also became more sophisticated consumers of the data, which created a positive spiral for more evaluation, as Sonnichsen (2000) predicted.

Lack of Skill

Expertise can be a problem. Sonnichsen (2000) identifies a critical organizational condition to be one in which evaluators are organizationally experienced, career employees, to which I would add that they also need to have the methodological and interpersonal skills. In my experience I've seen both ends of the spectrum. Generally, when starting a new function government organizations will move existing staff into the positions with the hopes that on-the-job training will be sufficient. I have seen this action in over 10 agencies I've consulted to. I've also observed agencies recruit and hire experts who are technically proficient, but so focused on the methodological that they miss the practical or have difficulty, as technical specialists, conveying data to decision makers in ways decision makers need. I've been asked by senior leaders in a few agencies to not include particular internal evaluators at meetings because the evaluators didn't have the political savvy or communication skills to work well at that level. Additionally, to be successful we had to master skills in addition to knowing social science research methodology and quantitative and qualitative analysis. We had to be equally as good in project management, to ensure projects were delivered in a reasonable amount of time and on or under budget; contract management, to oversee the contracts with external evaluators to know what was allowable and what wasn't; knowledge management, to know how to organize, store, and retrieve data from a variety of sources; and marketing and public relations, to communicate findings to a wide audience in multiple formats and styles effectively and to understand how findings can be used and misused. I was blessed that the three core members of the team were a blend of well-balanced skills and personalities that complemented and supplemented each other into a well-rounded and balanced team.

Lack of Bills

Despite some popular misconceptions, federal budgets are finite, especially for evaluation. Resource allocation is about making trade-offs, and one of the most common issues regarding evaluation resources is leaders not wanting to reduce the scope of a program to fund a backward-looking study they don't have confidence will tell them anything useful. I found that there are only two ways to increase the size of the evaluation resources: cost savings by being more efficient, and using the alternative skills mentioned above to create the value proposition. When leaders trust and rely on information, and it meets multiple needs, they will be far more likely to support it. For better or worse, we operate in a political environment, and egos can come into play, which means that if evaluation makes the organization (and the leader) look good to their stakeholders and peers, it becomes indispensable. This does not mean that evaluation sells out, or compromises integrity, but instead, an evaluation "posture" is created that shows the leader is knowledgeable about all that is within his or her responsibility and that management by fact or data is used and can be articulated by the leader. Helping the leader be a better manager through evaluation became an essential skill.

Lack of Fill

This refers to the disconnect between evaluation and other data reposito-ries. Because data needs are usually not discussed in an enterprise-wide way, it leads many agencies to develop independent application systems and/or data storage. Although this is changing, primarily from an information tech-nology investment standpoint and advances in shared computing concepts, I still find evaluators absent from the table. In our case, a successful evalu-ation had to draw upon data from the program office, the program partners, the grants coordination office, the budget office, and the U.S. embassies, yet none of these data pieces were captured in a single place. And, different pro-grams within ECA used different terminology (or taxonomies), making it difficult to align data. For example, the term "grantee" in one program referred to the individual participant, and in another was used to reference the institution that held the grant to implement the project. I also run across a number of agencies where the performance measurement function is com-pletely separated from the evaluation function to the degree that there is no alignment of the data, which can lead to duplication efforts, or data incon-sistencies. To overcome this lack, I believe the key is to collocate data ware-housing functions with evaluation, or at a minimum, ensure that an internal evaluator with expertise in data management is a part of regular data orga-nization, storage, and usage discussions.

Evaluation Kill: Shelf-Life or Half-Life

How evaluations are communicated can end an evaluation function quickly. Shelf-life refers to those evaluations that may be technically accurate, may have incredibly valuable data, but are communicated in a way that doesn't resonate with decision makers and end up sitting on shelves or being used as doorstops (Winberg, 1991). As I used to tell some of our external evalu-ators, a pair of graphs can be more powerful than a paragraph. We often spent a third of the project time on evaluations editing reports to make them readable and targeted to our program managers and leaders. We found many reports to be verbose and with key points buried so that the report didn't convey what decision makers needed to know quickly. One senior manager told me that if evaluations didn't "sing," meaning he couldn't get the main point, or at least become interested in continuing to read from an evalua-tion in 30 seconds or less, we had failed. Evaluation half-life, on the other end, were those reports that were written without any sensitivity to the political environment in which programs operate and thus were deemed "radioactive" by leaders. These are the reports that are never released for fear of the great damage it might cause the agency. The key to overcoming these constraints is, once again, to understand the needs and styles of the audiences and to be able to talk to them in their language. This doesn't mean that as evaluators we can't speak truth to power, but instead, we can be tactful and sensitive to how to convey that information. It also means knowing when to convey information. In a few cases, we separated out the management issues from the outcome assessment and provided a separate special report to the program leaders as an internal document. We often viewed our evaluation reports, or their summaries, as an informational piece to explain the features and benefits of a program (Office of Policy and Evaluation, ECA, 2011), and where we were targeting improvement efforts to make it even better.

The Counsel: Implications for Internal Evaluation

Through my evaluation survival journey, I discovered that for internal government evaluation to be successful, it had to be redefined in a number of ways.

The evaluator's responsibility for being inclusive is critical. It is incumbent upon the evaluator to ensure that all voices are heard and included in the process. The extent to which evaluation is inclusive or participatory is up to the evaluator's training and comfort, but without a strong collaborative process, internal evaluation builds resistance instead of results, as seen in ECA's evaluation history. The need for a collaborative, inclusive approach, described well by Sonnichsen, Emison, and the GAO, was the critical element for our transformation.

Evaluation must be a high-performing program, or professional service, with documented and communicated customer-focused vision, mission, and values; self-assessment; effective leadership; an engaged/empowered workforce; systems of planning, measurement, analysis, and knowledge management; process improvement, identifiable, measurable results, and a learning and feedback loop (Federal Quality Institute, 1994). Most importantly, internal evaluators must be adept at many management skills and intangible leadership qualities, so they will be embraced as trusted advisors and not dismissed as an administrative task.

Evaluators need to be accountable examiners of context. Quantifying impact is unlikely to diminish as an expectation for evaluators, but internal evaluators can bring context to numbers, and through tools like logic models can better explain the theories of change and action underlying programs, and move understanding and discussion from strictly causation to plausible attribution and contribution. Internal evaluators can be the interpreters and translators between stakeholders and program managers, between researchers and practitioners, between politicals and careerists.

Evaluation needs to be a continual process to help the organization learn, and thus better adapt to its future. Of nearly all the functional areas I've seen in government, internal evaluators have the potential for the widest access to all functions and levels within an organization to help to bring them together, align strategy and execution, and help organizations truly become more effective and efficient. Evaluators should strive to be the hub of organizational networking and excellence.

References

Brache, A. P. (2002). *How organizations work: Taking a holistic approach to enterprise health.* New York, NY: John Wiley & Sons, Inc.

Emison, G. A. (2007). *Practical program evaluation.* Washingon, DC: CQ Press.

Federal Quality Institute. (1994). *Creating a customer-driven government.* Washington, DC: Federal Quality Institute.

GAO. (2003). *Program evaluation: An evaluation culture and collaborative partnerships help build agency capacity.* Washington, DC: GAO.

Kirkpatrick, D. L., & Kirkpatrick, J. D. (2006). *Evaluating training programs: The four levels* (3rd ed.). San Francisco, CA: Berrett-Koehler.

Love, A. J. (1991). *Internal evaluation: Building organizations from within.* Newbury Park, CA: Sage.

National Institute of Standards and Technology. (2011, July). *Criteria for performance excellence.* Retrieved from: Baldrige Home Page: http://www.nist.gov/baldrige /publications/business_nonprofit_criteria.cfm

Office of Management and Budget. (2008, November). *Global educational and cultural exchange.* Retrieved from: Expect More: http://www.expectmore.gov

Office of Policy and Evaluation, ECA. (2011, July). *Completed program evaluations.* Retrieved from: Bureau of Educational and Cultural Affairs—Exchanges: http:// exchanges.state.gov/programevaluations/completed.html

Performance Breakthroughs, Inc. (2011, July). *High performance organizations overview.* Retrieved from: Performance Breakthroughs: http://www.performancebreak-throughs.com/high-performance-organizations/high-performance-organizations-overview.html

Sonnichsen, R. C. (2000). *High impact internal evaluation.* Thousand Oaks, CA: Sage.

U.S. Department of State. (2011, July 11). *About the bureau-exchanges.* Retrieved from: Bureau of Educational and Cultural Affairs-Exchanges: http://exchanges.state .gov/about.html

U.S. Office of Personnel Management. (2011, July). *PMF/about us/policy.* Retrieved from: PMF: http://www.pmf.gov/about-us/policy.aspx

Winberg, A. (1991). Maximizing the contribution of internal evaluation units. *Evaluation and Program Planning, 14,* 167–172.

Wolloch, C., & Siegel, J. (1998). *History of ECA evaluation.* (T. Kniker, interviewer).

TED KNIKER *is the executive director of the Performance Institute, and previously served as director of consulting services for the U.S. Department of the Interior's Federal Consulting Group and chief of evaluation and performance measurement for the U.S. Department of State's Bureau of Educational and Cultural Affairs and Public Diplomacy Office of Planning, Policy and Resources.*

King, J. A., & Rohmer-Hirt, J. A. (2011). Internal evaluation in American public school districts: The importance of externally driven accountability mandates. In B. B. Volkov & M. E. Baron (Eds.), *Internal evaluation in the 21st century. New Directions for Evaluation*, 132, 73–86.

6

Internal Evaluation in American Public School Districts: The Importance of Externally Driven Accountability Mandates

Jean A. King, Johnna A. Rohmer-Hirt

Abstract

From the 1980s to the present, educational accountability in the United States has grown dramatically. Such accountability in U.S. school districts, although driven primarily by external demands, has internal manifestations as well. The chapter traces the historical development of internal evaluation in American school districts, then highlights four current forms of internal evaluation (standardized testing programs, evaluations of externally funded programs, support for school improvement planning, and evaluation capacity building), along with a brief description of the decade-long development of internal evaluation in one school district. The unique features of internal evaluation in educational settings are highlighted, and the chapter concludes with implications of current practice for the continuing development of internal educational evaluation. © Wiley Periodicals, Inc., and the American Evaluation Association.

The unique requirements of a particular sector affect the form and viability of internal evaluation. This chapter discusses the current practice of internal evaluation in public school districts in the United States under difficult conditions anticipated by Love (1983) nearly 30 years ago. ". . . [I]n times of economic turbulence," he argued, "the internal evaluation process is essential for survival, because it provides the information crucial for program improvement, accountability, and planned change under adverse circumstances" (p. 5). In American public education today, school boards and district administrators often face the continuing challenge of finding resources to sustain meaningful evaluation efforts over time, given the competing pressures of accountability, efficiency, and the imperative of increasing achievement for all students while simultaneously closing the achievement gap for students traditionally at risk of failure. As escalating accountability and declining financial resources confront contemporary public education in the United States, departments of testing, research, and evaluation by whatever names may well lack the means to evaluate ongoing programs routinely, even as ". . . the benefits of the evaluation process are being recognized as useful to organizations as they confront the dilemma of performance demands, information overload, and reduced resources" (Sonnichsen, 2000, p. 33).

The chapter will first trace the historical development of internal evaluation in American school districts. Highlighting four activities, it will next present the forms that district internal evaluation currently takes, along with a brief description of the roughly decade-long development of the internal evaluation unit of one school district. The third section will identify what makes internal evaluation in educational settings unique, and the chapter will conclude with implications of this current practice for internal educational evaluation. The chapter will not address the legislative issues associated with public education funding or with internal evaluation within state and federal education agencies, as they are beyond its scope.

A Brief History of Internal Educational Evaluation in the United States

Educational accountability, according to Nevo (2001), can be "traced back to the long tradition of controlling schools by means of external evaluation" (p. 96). Owing to state and district control of public education in the United States, the 19th-century tradition of British school inspection did not directly translate to educational practice in this country. By contrast, the development of school accreditation at the beginning of the 20th century was primarily a voluntary commitment of individual school leaders to ensure the standardization not of student outcomes, but of resources and processes. The eventual development of nationwide goals for education in the first half of the century (e.g., the Cardinal Principles of Secondary Education in 1918, What the High Schools Ought to Teach in 1940) pointed to common learning deemed desirable, but without a commitment or mandate to measuring its successful achievement. With the increasing availability of standardized measures of student achievement, districts voluntarily began to measure certain academic goals with the use of standardized tests. Typically, students were tested at certain points during their precollegiate academic careers, and the results were used as indicators of district effectiveness; there were few direct consequences for students, schools, or districts.

Simultaneously, the field of program evaluation originated "in the projects" (Patton, 2008, p. 14)—the federal antipoverty and education programs of the 1960s, including Head Start and Follow Through, among others. Federal funding mandated school-district participation in large-scale evaluations of these programs. Indeed, Fitzpatrick, Sanders, and Worthen (2011, pp. 44–55) identify the evaluation provisions of the Elementary and Secondary Education Act (ESEA) of 1965 as the key event in the development of program evaluation as a field. In the 1960s and 1970s larger school districts created offices in the central administration to manage these mandatory federal evaluations and expanding testing programs (King, 2003); smaller districts typically assigned an individual these responsibilities. The launch of the National Assessment of Educational Progress (NAEP) in 1964 and its first assessments in 1969 began an ongoing assessment of "what America's students know and can do in various subject areas" (NAEP, 2011) that continues to this day.

From the 1980s to the present, educational accountability in the United States has grown dramatically. As McNamara and O'Hara (2008) note, "One result of these policies [to ensure accountability] has been that virtually every education system in the developed world and indeed many others elsewhere have been busy creating or where they existed before reforming their school evaluation policies and procedures" (p. 173). Nevo's (2001) "long tradition of controlling schools by means of external evaluation" has taken a uniquely American shape, and both technological and psychometric developments have supported the demand for public accountability. The addition of highly visible consequences for states and school districts through The Goals 2000: Educate America Act in 1994 and the eventual renaming of the federal Elementary and Secondary Education Act as No Child Left Behind (NCLB) in 2002 have greatly increased public attention on test results in area schools, which are routinely published in local newspapers. "In many cases, . . . accountability strategies or tools are the central vehicles for reform, on the assumption that holding schools, parents and students accountable for attaining higher standards will trigger schools to improve their quality" (Blok, Sleegers, & Karsten, 2008, pp. 379–380).

The effects of the NCLB legislation on districts' internal evaluation systems have been striking, requiring the mandated testing of all students, grades 3–8, and selected grades in high school (rather than a sample of students in certain grades), and the documentation of adequate yearly progress (AYP) for all students, schools, and districts (Pub. L. 107–110, 2002). Special needs students and those who are English language learners are included in testing procedures, and districts are held accountable for their test results as well. "[W]ithin the U.S. context, educational accountability is constructed as AYP on large-scale assessments overall and by subgroups. How exactly the particular numbers represented by AYP denote educational effectiveness and what kind of effectiveness are largely ignored . . . The current wave of educational accountability is relegated to an audit function disconnected from improving teaching and learning" (Ryan, 2005, p. 535). Schools whose student groups fail to make adequate yearly progress suffer a series of increasingly dire consequences, resulting finally in the school's reconstitution. It is important to note that, although most educators appear to agree in theory with the transition in focus from calculating averages to attending to individual student performance, there is considerable disagreement with the sanctions and unfunded mandates associated with the legislation. This chapter will not, however, center on the debate over the federal accountability legislation.

In addition and by contrast, powerful developments in available technology have increasingly enabled districts to collect, analyze, and use assessment data to support individual student learning. Thanks to decreased cost and increased functionality and accessibility, many classroom teachers have access to achievement information on their current students, rather than on the students they taught in previous years. Many are also able to administer diagnostic tests that enable them to target instruction to the individual needs of specific students routinely. With the use of data, building administrators can now identify teachers whose students are learning the mandated curriculum and those whose students are struggling. Building-level school improvement plans routinely unite faculty around annual achievement goals and targeted instruction to reach them.

In the first decades of the 21st century, then, educational accountability in U.S. school districts, while driven primarily by external demands, has internal manifestations as well. Nevertheless, the following statement, written almost a decade ago, remains true: "In the context of a school district in the United States, at least for the foreseeable future, program evaluation will remain secondary to administering standardized tests and reporting their results" (King, 2002, p. 78).

Components of Internal Evaluation in U.S. School Districts

In the past decade the demands of external accountability legislation have exerted profound influence on the internal evaluation processes of American school districts. State testing has expanded in complexity, the number of assessments administered has grown, and the severity of consequences imposed for not meeting set targets has increased. Districts and schools have responded to accountability measures put in place to monitor achievement progress and to determine effectiveness. Internally, these measures have prompted several developments—an impetus to focus on every child's progression instead of on district averages, a more systemic approach to learning aligned with standards, and, in many districts, more meaningful strategic planning. These developments have also impelled districts to create structures and processes to support the collection of multiple types of data, to make data more easily accessible, and to deliver professional development focused on understanding and interpreting data and on data-informed decision making. The sheer amount of mandatory assessment, aligned and connected to accountability, has the ability to overwhelm the activities of internal evaluation offices, completely dominating departmental staff time. Internal evaluation in school districts currently has four primary components, each of which will be briefly discussed: extensive programs of standardized testing, the mandated evaluations of externally funded programs, support for school improvement processes, and, in some cases, efforts to build evaluation capacity.

A Program of Standardized Testing

Standardized testing programs, the first component of internal evaluation, include state-mandated tests in various subjects and district-initiated tests, both to comply with NCLB requirements and to provide teachers useful data on individual students. For these data to be fully beneficial, districts need a comprehensive assessment system that includes defined curriculum, standardized assessments, and formative and summative common assessments that teachers can use to shape instruction.

Defining a district-wide curriculum helps to assure that all students are given the same opportunities to a guaranteed and viable curriculum aligned with standards against which they will be measured and held accountable. Identifying essential learner outcomes at the program, course, unit, and lesson level can provide a basis to monitor student progress related to the standards. Identifying common misunderstandings, necessary vocabulary, and differentiation options helps further refine instruction and learning, especially for teachers unfamiliar with a particular course, thus negating the potential barrier of inexperience.

The administration of standardized assessments has huge implications for schools, districts, and their internal evaluation and testing departments in terms of time, attention, and continuous communication and training. The state of Minnesota, for example, began by requiring a handful of tests; over the last 10 years requirements have grown to include 96 different assessments (considering grade level, subject, and test type), including three high-stakes tests for students to determine graduation eligibility in writing, reading, and math, but not including the retests for each of these high-stakes assessments. In addition to legislatively required state assessments, district-initiated standardized assessments can guide instruction, identify individual student needs, and establish predictive models for accountability tests. Districts may also administer a host of college readiness assessments.

Along with the plethora of standardized assessments, districts often develop common formative and summative assessments, as well as supporting staff in the creation and use of ongoing formative assessments within classrooms, all aligned to standards and essential learner outcomes.

NEW DIRECTIONS FOR EVALUATION • DOI: 10.1002/ev

In larger districts item analysis may be conducted, as assessments are written and predictability studies performed to help assure the reliability and validity of these assessments.

Evaluations of Externally Funded Programs

The second component of internal district evaluation involves evaluations of externally funded programs. Examples of such programs include those targeting specific student populations related to race, socioeconomic status, living conditions (for example, migrant or homeless circumstances); students acquiring English language; and students involved in science, technology, engineering and math (STEM) initiatives, all related to accountability and equitable educational access for all students. With declining resources, funding is increasingly moving away from entitlement allocations and diverted into competitive grants. These grants force districts to participate in or conduct formal program evaluations, which is frequently an accountability requirement of grant acceptance. Many working in districts may perceive evaluations done for this purpose as less an internally informative practice and more an external hoop to jump through.

Support for School Improvement Processes

Legislative accountability has spurred many districts to develop more formal school improvement processes to monitor and predict student performance against identified standards, the third component in internal district evaluation. Routinely, evaluation and testing department staff, central or building administrators, or teacher leaders lead broad-scale meetings that bring together a wide range of stakeholders. At these meetings people examine previous plans and data related to past performance. From such analyses, staff develop new goals, usually SMART goals (strategic, measurable, attainable, results-based, and time-bound), acknowledge challenge areas, craft action plans including progress measurements to achieve these goals, and identify related professional development needs. These school improvement plans, as they are called, are sometimes only for internal use, but, in the case of schools and districts facing accountability sanctions, state-level review is often mandatory.

Other improvement efforts that occur within districts include action research, many times associated with staff pursuing advanced degrees or piloting innovative means of instruction, and data-informed decision making (also commonly referred to as data-driven or data-based decision making), which, in relation to internal evaluation, should be "a management tool designed to furnish unbiased information that improves decisions, not a mechanism for decision justification" (Sonnichsen, 2000, p. 21).

Building Evaluation Capacity

A fourth component in district-level internal evaluation involves the purposeful development of evaluation capacity—evaluation capacity building

NEW DIRECTIONS FOR EVALUATION • DOI: 10.1002/ev

(ECB). Sonnichsen (2000) writes that "the ultimate objective [of internal evaluation] is to build evaluation capacity in the organization to an acceptable level where evaluation is perceived as an indispensible component in the structural, administrative and operational configuration of the organization" (p. 18). Building a culture of evaluative thinking means that staff not only have the desire to embrace and use evaluation findings, but they gain the capacity to conduct further evaluation with the support of an internal evaluation unit. ECB activities often mean engaging staff in evaluations, teaching them the process as they take part over the course of an evaluation study. Thus, evaluation capacity building is a way to augment program evaluation in districts without extensive resources to hire professional evaluators. Focus on context, infrastructure, and resources can help build capacity over time (Volkov & King, 2007).

One District's Story

The development of internal evaluation in one district points to dramatic changes in practice over the past decade. As a district, Anoka-Hennepin (Minnesota) Independent District No. 11[1] has valued evaluation for decades, for example, requiring a high school graduation test many years before the state-mandated one and playing a leadership role in performance assessment statewide in the 1990s. Comparing the Department of Research and Evaluation activities from 1999 to 2001 (King, 2002) with those of the Department of Research, Evaluation, and Testing 10 years later points to dramatic changes in routine evaluation practice in the district, including departmental significance within the district.

At the turn of the 21st century, test data were hard to access, there was extremely limited technology in classrooms, and the only formal evaluations were those of externally funded programs, routinely conducted by external evaluators. Standardized achievement tests were unrelated to the district's curriculum, and at best teachers received test data on their previous year's students in the middle of the fall. Staffing at that time included a district assessment/testing coordinator and a temporary Director of Research and Evaluation, funded on soft money. (In 2000, budget constraints prevented hiring a full-time director to supervise an expanding Evaluation, Assessment, and Research Department.) In the 2 years that the temporary Director worked in the district, the district's evaluation capacity did increase through highly visible evaluations of the state's graduation rule and the special education department, the purposeful development of a data-collection and analysis infrastructure, and an increased focus on school improvement processes (King, 2002).

With the reauthorization of the Elementary Secondary Education Act as No Child Left Behind, however, all activity in the Research and Evaluation Department turned to a focus on testing and on understanding the implications of this new level of accountability. The following years were spent implementing district-initiated standardized tests aligned to external accountability measures, understanding state standards and performance-level expectations, creating systems and processes to ensure data accuracy and security, acquiring technological tools, and training staff to grasp the meaning and use of the data.

Fast forward to 2011, and the status of internal evaluation in the district has changed dramatically. The renamed Department of Research, Evaluation, and Testing has transitioned from an auxiliary role with limited access to the upper echelon to a leading role in strategic planning and program performance measurement on the instructional side of the organization, with strengthening inroads to the district's operational side and direct access to top district leadership, as well as routine inclusion in organizational discussion and decision making. Numerous changes point to the stable infrastructure supporting internal evaluation work:

> There is a full-time Director of Research, Evaluation, and Testing, as well as increased evaluation staffing in the central office, including a full-time measurement expert, a full-time psychometrician, and several staff dedicated to supporting evaluation and data use across the district.
>
> District curriculum is now aligned to standards measured by local, state, and national standardized tests. Professional Learning Communities (PLCs) and collaborative teams (CTs), providing on-going job-embedded staff development and collegial sharing, are common in buildings at all levels.
>
> There are software and tools available for teachers to access and analyze existing data on their current students, as well as longitudinal and trend data.
>
> Strategic planning, goal setting at the district, building, grade and collaborative team levels, action plan writing and other forms of school improvement incorporate and build on the data collected for accountability purposes.

In addition, system-wide staff development is aligned with improvement plans. Thanks to federal stimulus dollars, district staff are working to increase and sustain evaluation capacity district-wide, picking up from what was started 10 years ago, then halted—creating a program evaluation model aligned to district beliefs and philosophy.

What Distinguishes Internal Evaluation in American School Districts?

At this time, external mandates of two types are primarily responsible for determining the internal "evaluation" agenda for U.S. school districts' evaluation offices:

NEW DIRECTIONS FOR EVALUATION • DOI: 10.1002/ev

1. The Mandated Testing Requirements of NCLB

It is important to note that standardized testing programs are not program evaluations *per se*. They measure student outcomes directly, but without grounding in descriptions of the multiple variables of the educational programs that may have generated them. A testing program is a program evaluation only in its broadest sense, that is, where the combined activities of an entire district, grade by grade, constitute the "program" and the test outcomes allow people to judge district and school effectiveness as a result.

Testing programs are, however, the dominant form of "evaluation" in most American school districts in this decade. As discussed above, testing has increased greatly under NCLB. These tests focus on assessing student learning in core subject areas, and district evaluation offices (if they exist) are in charge of the many tasks related to ordering, distributing, administering, and ultimately packing test materials for shipping to wherever they will be scored, in addition to preparing the annual internal and public reports for release when the scores are returned and facilitating processes for internal use of the data. In many districts the resources required to manage testing programs may well limit funds that could be spent on activities more directly related to instruction. The inclusion of *all* children in NCLB testing—for example, those with special needs and English language learners—has increased the need for test accommodations and for alternative and modified forms that more accurately measure outcomes for certain types of students; such changes increase the costs of the testing program even if state departments of education pay to develop appropriate procedures.

School districts must pay close attention to NCLB testing, as there are serious consequences for many—school board members, administrators, teachers, and students among them—when the public perceives the results as inadequate. The political challenges facing board members, central office administrators, and principals when schools fail to make adequate yearly progress can be nightmarish, including the potential loss of their jobs. Teachers can also be affected. Those who may have viewed "teaching to the test" (targeted instruction on material to be tested) negatively in the past may well increase such instruction with the advent of value-added measurements that link student outcomes to that year's instructors. Students unable to pass a high school graduation test will not receive the diploma that affects their lifelong earning potential and may well be placed in remedial classes or other intervention activities both during and outside the school day and outside the school year. Given the visibility of district and individual schools' test results as well as their potential high stakes for students, the importance of effectively managing these tests in district offices cannot be overstated.

2. Mandated Evaluations of Programs Receiving External Funding

The second area where external mandates create agenda items for districts' internal evaluation activities relates to externally funded programs, that is, when funding from the federal or state government or from grants dictates, as a condition of funding, what programs must be evaluated. These are the strings that accompany such external funding, and, in many districts, these studies may be the only consistent examples of routine program evaluations. In a sense, the periodic curricular reviews required by state departments of education are a special example of such mandated program evaluations.

The fact that *external* mandates drive district agendas for *internal* "evaluation"—and, again, a testing program is a program evaluation only in its broadest sense—highlights a critical distinction of educational program evaluation at this point in the history of American education. By and large these evaluation activities are conducted in the highly visible arena of district or state politics, engaging school boards, superintendents, and central office personnel in public conversations about how to improve educational practice that will lead to improved outcomes.

At the district level, the concerns of central office administrators and board members differ from the needs of their internal evaluators. First, eager to avoid negative press, superintendents and board members typically pay close attention to media relations. Second, although they may not necessarily understand research methods and data analyses, they need to have research grounding and data to support their decisions because that is now considered "best practice." Third, they need to know what causes what and often demand straightforward answers, easily understood and without nuance, to complex questions of causation: What reading program will increase test scores next year? What interventions will improve outcomes for special needs students across the district? What were the differential effects of that remedial math program? How can the district close the achievement gap that appears to increase over time despite best efforts to the contrary? Fourth, they also need these answers in a timely manner, which often means quickly and occasionally with timelines that are technically impossible. As Lisa Jones, former internal evaluator for a large urban district, puts it, "There is a tension between the time we need to do an evaluation—evaluation time—and political time. [The superintendent says,] 'I need an answer for Tuesday's Board meeting'" (L. Jones, personal communication, 2011). Finally, the use of resources to support program evaluation is itself an evaluative question: Is it better to pay for an evaluator or for a classroom teacher? Central office administrators and board members may find it difficult to expand evaluation resources when class sizes rise above 30 or 35 or a sizeable number of teachers must be laid off for budgetary reasons.

Not surprisingly, the concerns of internal evaluators are different. Because they are not elected officials and do not serve at the will of a school board, their positions are not vulnerable when the results of tests or evaluation studies are disappointing. Their job is to administer the district's testing and evaluation program, whatever activities that includes, and to help prepare and deliver both internal and public reports based on the results of testing and evaluation. A key concern is that everyone involved—both inside and outside the district—perceive them as objective, credible, and unengaged in political turmoil; perceived objectivity is typically more readily attributed to external evaluators, especially in the presence of contentious or litigious situations (Conley-Tyler, 2005; Love, 1998). The district's internal evaluators embody the technical competencies related to systematic inquiry, data-collection methods, analytical techniques, and the appropriate interpretation of results. As Jim Angermeyr, long-time evaluator for a suburban district, recently noted, "You have to be sure that you don't really care what the results are. As soon as your bias is evident, you lose your credibility" (J. Angermeyr, personal communication, March 2011). In the tension between "evaluation time" and "political time," evaluators must ensure their decision makers the highest-quality evaluation information possible in a timely manner, standing firm in the face of impossible or unethical demands that would yield inaccurate data or conclusions.

Throughout, they must serve as the technical experts, ensuring that the data are not misinterpreted, inaccurate conclusions reached, unhappy results willfully eliminated, and so on. The challenge is to provide appropriate, nuanced "answers" that do not misrepresent the data, especially when their internal clients are seeking simple answers to complex questions. The output of Google searches and simple research summaries in practitioner journals provide insufficient preparation for district leaders, and they may well rely on their evaluators to teach them what the data mean. Often with limited access or time to do so, internal evaluators must help district administrators and perhaps board members (whose positions may be vulnerable) to use data appropriately, for example, to cite them accurately or to understand intricate analyses.

Implications for Internal Educational Evaluation

Even as external mandates in many districts consume sizeable portions of evaluation resources, there are increasingly, as noted previously, forms of internal evaluation that engage school-based practitioners with data to change practice. School improvement planning is commonplace at the school level, and technology has made data of multiple types available at the classroom level, providing teachers data on their current students in real time. The challenge for internal district evaluators is to support processes—often with limited resources and often outside their realm of professional responsibility—to help principals and teachers use test data effectively. The increasing development of professional learning communities, in which groups of teachers come together around data or design action research efforts, holds the potential to systematize the process of program evaluation (framing questions, taking an action, collecting and reflecting on data, and then reconsidering) to improve instruction for individual students. Integrating educational evaluators into these processes holds the potential to develop the role of internal evaluator described in the existing literature

(Clifford & Sherman, 1983; Kyriakides & Campbell, 2004; Love, 1991; Mathison, 1991; Sonnichsen, 2000).

Almost 30 years ago Clifford and Sherman (1983) noted that to promote change the internal evaluator needs professional and technical credibility and access to the top, supplying their intended users with useful information. In school districts internal evaluators can build on their knowledge of school improvement to conduct high-quality evaluations with reasonable timelines and sufficient support, consistently advocating for the resources needed for this work. They face the challenge of having one foot squarely in each of two worlds: the political environment of a public school district, and the professional world of educational evaluation. In the first, political pressures may frustrate their efforts to explain the intricate details of complex analyses. In the words of Lisa Jones: "Simplicity is sexy. What we [evaluators] do and say isn't sexy. 'It depends' is not sexy. Decision makers want the answers" (L. Jones, personal communication, 2011). Thankfully, in the second, the increasing professionalism of the field of program evaluation provides a number of resources, including the Program Evaluation Standards (Joint Committee, 2011) and the Guiding Principles of the American Evaluation Association, enabling evaluators to frame their "it depends" comments in the context of professional practice.

In an environment of declining resources, the combination of mandates for external accountability and the need for continuous improvement provide a strong basis for internal evaluation in school districts. Although external mandates have to date largely driven the agenda for internal evaluation in districts, support for internal evaluation ". . . will be forthcoming if internal evaluators can regularly demonstrate that the information they produce is useful, adds value to the organization's operations, and justifies the resources allocated to the evaluation process" (Sonnichsen, 2000, p. 5). Evaluation specialists within school districts can combine the strengths attributed to both internal and external evaluators, leading to the best possible institutional evaluation outcomes while simultaneously building the evaluation capacity of the districts within which they work. Ryan (2005, p. 537) even proposes that educational evaluators engage in *democratic accountability* (Ryan, 2004), a new form of accountability through which

> . . . parents, students, citizens, professionals (teachers and administrators), and experts join in dialogue and discussion . . . This kind of conversation creates a self-monitoring community that is committed to examining the implementation of school programs in general, in relationship to external accountability information, and in relationship to current educational policy.

Internal educational evaluation may, finally, have the ability to combine the best of all worlds: accountability, rigor, relevance, strategic planning, and continuous improvement.

Note

1. Anoka-Hennepin Independent School District No. 11 is now the largest school district in Minnesota, incorporating over 13 communities. It currently educates nearly 40,000 students, with approximately 22% students of color (up from 8% in the past decade), 12% of students qualifying for special education services (up from 11%), 32% of students qualifying for economic assistance (up from 14%), and 6% of students qualifying for English language acquisition services from 64 reported primary language variations (up from 2%).

References

Blok, H., Sleegers, P., & Karsten, S. (2008). Looking for a balance between internal and external evaluation of school quality: Evaluation of the SVI model. *Journal of Educational Policy, 23*(4), 379–395.

Clifford, D. L., & Sherman, P. (1983). Internal evaluation: Integrating program evaluation and management. *New Directions for Program Evaluation, 20,* 23–45.

Conley-Tyler, M. (2005). A fundamental choice: Internal or external evaluation? *Evaluation Journal of Australia, 9*(1 & 2), 3–11.

Fitzpatrick, J. L., Sanders, J. R., & Worthen, B. R. (2011). *Program evaluation: Alternative approaches and practical guidelines* (4th ed.). Boston, MA: Pearson.

Joint Committee on Educational Evaluation (2011). The program evaluation standards (3rd ed.). Thousand Oaks, CA: Sage.

King, J. A. (2002). Building evaluation capacity in a school district. *New Directions for Evaluation, 93,* 63–80.

King, J. A. (2003). Evaluating educational programs and projects in the USA. *International handbook of educational evaluation* (pp. 721–732). Dordrecht, Netherlands: Kluwer Academic.

Kyriakides, L., & Campbell, R. J. (2004). School self-evaluation and school improvement: A critique of values and procedures. *Studies in Educational Evaluation, 30,* 23–36.

Love, A. J. (1983). The organizational context and the development of internal evaluation. *New Directions for Program Evaluation, 20,* 5–22.

Love, A. J. (1991). *Internal evaluation: Building organizations from within.* Newbury Park, CA: Sage.

Love, A. J. (1998). Internal evaluation: Integrating evaluation and social work practice. *Scandinavian Journal of Social Welfare, 7,* 145–151.

Mathison, S. (1991). What do we know about internal evaluation? *Evaluation and Program Planning, 14,* 159–165.

McNamara, G., & O'Hara, J. (2008). The importance of the concept of self-evaluation in the changing landscape of educational policy. *Studies in Educational Evaluation, 34,* 173–179.

National Assessment of Educational Progress. (2011). Retrieved from http://nces.ed.gov/nationsreportcard/about/

Nevo, D. (2001). School evaluation: Internal or external? *Studies in Educational Evaluation, 27,* 95–106.

Patton, M. Q. (2008). *Utilization-focused evaluation* (4th ed.). Thousand Oaks, CA: Sage.

Pub. L. 107–110, § 1111, 115 Stat. 1450 and § 1116, 115 Stat. 1465 (January 8, 2002).

Ryan, K. E. (2004). Serving public interest in educational accountability: Alternative approaches to democratic evaluation. *American Journal of Evaluation, 25*(4), 443–460.

Ryan, K. E. (2005). Making educational accountability more democratic. *American Journal of Evaluation, 26*(4), 532–543.

Sonnichsen, R. C. (2000). *High impact internal evaluation: A practitioner's guide to evaluating and consulting inside organizations.* Thousand Oaks, CA: Sage.

Volkov, B., & King, J. A. (2007). *A checklist for building organizational evaluation capacity.* The Evaluation Center: Western Michigan University. Retrieved from http://www.wmich.edu/evalctr/checklists/ecb.pdf

JEAN A. KING is a professor and director of graduate studies in the Department of Organizational Leadership, Policy, and Development at the University of Minnesota.

JOHNNA A. ROHMER-HIRT is the director of the Research, Evaluation, and Testing Office at Anoka-Hennepin Independent School District No. 11 and an evaluation studies doctoral student in the Department of Organizational Leadership, Policy, and Development at the University of Minnesota.

NEW DIRECTIONS FOR EVALUATION • DOI: 10.1002/ev

Baron, M. E. (2011). Designing internal evaluation for a small organization with limited resources. In B. B. Volkov & M. E. Baron (Eds.), *Internal evaluation in the 21st century.* *New Directions for Evaluation, 132,* 87–99.

7

Designing Internal Evaluation for a Small Organization With Limited Resources

Michelle E. Baron

Abstract

The chapter outlines strategies that small organizations at the early, midterm, and seasoned levels of evaluation capacity can cultivate, and offers some practical tips for evaluators on developing and maintaining internal evaluation within a small organization. The author deliberates that as organizational and evaluative skills work in tandem, members of the organization turn to the internal evaluator for support, are proactive in resolving program difficulties, and are open to future evaluations and capacity-building efforts. © Wiley Periodicals, Inc., and the American Evaluation Association.

Evaluation capacity building (ECB) as a technique and evaluation itself as a helping profession have propagated throughout many disciplines and organizations (Preskill, 2008; Preskill & Boyle, 2008). The goal of ECB is "to continuously create and sustain overall organizational processes that make quality evaluation and its uses routine" (Baizerman, Compton, & Stockdill, 2002, p. 14). Internal evaluation processes and systems, as well as external ones, are required to make this goal a reality. "Evaluation has become a valuable commodity in modern society," writes Ernest House (House, 1986, p. 63) in his reflections on internal evaluation. "Administrators find evaluation too valuable to leave outside their agencies and too dangerous to be removed from administrative control. So they have created sizable evaluation staffs within their organizations" (p. 63). Thus begin the careers of many internal evaluators.

For the purposes of this article, internal evaluation is defined as "evaluation conducted by a staff member or unit from within the organization being studied" (The Evaluation Center, n.d.). An internal evaluator is defined as an employee of the organization who performs evaluation functions to any degree—whether alone or in conjunction with other duties and responsibilities.

Internal evaluation has flourished in such fields as government (Duffy, 1994; Mangano, 1992; Newcomer, 2004; Sonnichsen, 1987, 1990; Wye & Sonnichsen, 1992), business and industry (Morell, 2000; Nowakowski, 1989), medicine (Newman, Heverly, Rosen, Kopta, & Bedell, 1983), and education (Nevo, 1993; Smith & Freeman, 2002). The literature shows that large organizations have a distinct advantage when it comes to internal evaluation due to extensive resources available and opportunities for funding from numerous sources (Cummings et al., 1988; Lambur, 2008). Smaller organizations oftentimes may not have the resources or political influence to justify and support an evaluation staff or activities. Organizations' exposure to evaluation may be limited depending on the background and experience of the employees and leadership of the organization, the priority of evaluation within the goals of the organization, and the access to evaluation training and expertise.

No matter what the size of the organization, internal evaluation can be a prevalent, thriving activity that reaches beyond the political, economic, or social barriers to propel the organization forward. Regardless of the particular setting, internal evaluators can greatly improve the quality, efficiency, and effectiveness of programs and services. Being internal to the organization allows internal evaluators to have a bird's-eye view of the situation, and they can initiate evaluations when necessary as well as shape a proper direction for evaluation planning for the entire organization (Nowakowski, 1989).

After reviewing basic processes of ECB, and introducing a case-study example, this article will outline ways in which small organizations at the early, midterm, and seasoned levels of evaluation capacity can develop and maintain internal evaluation systems. Importantly, successful internal evaluation is a mind-set that can thrive in organizations regardless of size or resource limitations.

Building Internal Evaluation: A Lesson From Capacity Building

Building internal evaluation involves the creation and maintenance of an evaluation environment within the organization. "ECB is about learning how to think evaluatively and how to engage in sound evaluation practice" (Preskill & Boyle, 2008, p. 443). Internal evaluators can help to create evaluation capacity within their organization. To do so, the internal evaluator works with managers and other decision makers to help them see the importance of evaluation, to obtain the resources to conduct and utilize evaluations, and to create the structure and mind-set necessary to sustain evaluation within an organization. The internal evaluator teaches them to be aware of and conduct their own evaluations, and to use that information to improve their organizations and the programs, processes, products, and performances therein (Duignan, 2003; Preskill, 2008).

The internal evaluator may accomplish this by using the strategies and plans found in such a framework as the multidisciplinary model of evaluation capacity building (Preskill & Boyle, 2008). The internal evaluator should understand the knowledge, skills, and attitudes of the organization, and can then develop effective ECB strategies (e.g., coaching, training, meetings, technical assistance, communities of practice) and sustainable evaluation practices (e.g., resources dedicated to evaluation, shared evaluation beliefs and commitment, evaluation policies and procedures) that fit the organization's leadership and culture. Although the internal evaluator is usually the one to perform the evaluation design, data collection, analysis, and reporting, increasingly, part of the evaluator's job is to establish an evaluation mind-set among the rest of the organization. With an evaluation structure in place, the organization more effectively embraces evaluation and understands the connections among evaluations and the mission, vision, and goals of the organization (King, 2007).

Scenario Example: The Army Inspector General (AIG)

I served as a detailed inspector general in a regional office of the Army Inspector General (AIG). As such, I was part of an internal evaluation group that planned, conducted, and reported evaluations of federal programs to streamline business processes and increase operational efficiency. Although the military may not normally be considered a small organization as a whole, the groups within the military are typically small organizations operating within a local area or a designated entity. In this case, a regional IG office of eight people had command and control oversight of a six-state region comprising 7,000 people—reasonably small in military standards. Although the IG office was a separate group from the auditing department, the IG office worked in conjunction with auditors to review such topics as medical records maintenance, vehicle licensing, risk management, and physical fitness throughout the designated region. In addition to evaluating the given topic, the team also conducted teaching and training on the topic itself and how the subordinate organizations could evaluate their own progress. The team conducted evaluation capacity building within and among regional sites. I will refer to my experiences as an inspector general throughout the article.

Early Capacity: Establishing Credibility

As people implement a new business idea, there are many steps to take into account. These steps may include establishing the business entity, writing a business plan, acquiring licenses, hiring personnel, purchasing equipment, promoting the business through networking and other marketing techniques, and a host of other tasks. Evaluation is often the last thing on their minds. Notwithstanding, establishing a new business is a key time to start instilling evaluation into individuals and the organization. The idea of evaluation capacity building is to engrain evaluation into the everyday practice of the organization (Baizerman et al., 2002; Compton & Baizerman, 2007; Stockdill, Baizerman, & Compton, 2002; Taut, 2007). What better way to begin such an endeavor than to start from the ground up when a new business is established. As business owners and respective employees tie evaluation into their overall business goals, objectives, and strategies, they will be more likely to establish evaluation processes, conduct evaluations, and use the results (King, 2007; Taylor-Powell & Boyd, 2008).

As organizations establish evaluation offices and hire or train people as internal evaluators, of vital importance is the location and accessibility of that evaluation office. The evaluation office should be positioned near executives and senior staff, but be accessible enough so that all entities may receive assistance from them as necessary (Sporn, 1989). Doing so helps the evaluation group to gain credibility, disseminate evaluation results and recommendations, and have the teeth necessary to facilitate evaluation use. Evaluation at this stage tends to be more developmental and formative in nature (Clifford & Sherman, 1983), and capacity-building efforts focus on building evaluation into the mix, whereby the respective staff members together establish resources necessary for evaluating programs and processes.

The offices of the AIG are located at the respective regional headquarters, putting them in close proximity to the Commanding General (i.e., the CEO of the organization) and senior staff members. This facilitates coordination of evaluations and dissemination and use of evaluation results. Newly formed regional offices tend to focus on building good working relationships with the Commanding General and staff members to understand stakeholder goals and values surrounding military programs better.

Internal evaluators in similar small organizations may capitalize on the newness of the organization by developing constant interaction with its senior decision makers. Whether an organization is an office of 2, 10, or 50, evaluation needs to be discussed actively if it is to be prevalent throughout the organization's programs. Both internal evaluators and associated staff may want to take part in professional development opportunities in evaluation, so that the staff may familiarize themselves with the concept of evaluation and how it benefits their organization. In so doing, the evaluators may ensure that the staff has the necessary training.

Midterm Capacity: Balancing Evaluation and Capacity Building

Internal evaluators have a unique standing in the organization in that they are both advocates of evaluation growth and partners to those involved in

the day-to-day tasks. Once internal evaluators get their footing in the organization, they must seize the opportunity to "serve as a basis for organizational learning, detecting and solving problems, acting as a self-correcting
mechanism by stimulating debate and reflection among organizational
actors, and seeking alternative solutions to persistent problems" (Sonnichsen,
2000, p. 78). Internal evaluators must engrain themselves into the very fiber
of the organization to perform credibility, assistance, and change-agent functions (House, 1989; Sonnichsen, 1989). Becoming involved in the organizational culture allows the internal evaluator to build the evaluation
capacity of the organization by helping members of the organization to see
evaluation as a daily process, and to prevent or change bad habits and attitudes related to evaluation, such as ignoring stakeholders, performing cur-
sory evaluations to satisfy compliance issues, and failing to prioritize
evaluation in the organization.

In addition to its three primary functions of performing inspections
(i.e., conducting evaluations of military programs), providing technical
assistance (i.e., referrals to resources and points of contact for additional
subject matter expertise on a military program, regulation, or procedure),
and conducting investigations (i.e., investigating cases of inappropriate conduct, fraud, waste, and abuse), the AIG also has responsibility for teaching
and training (Office of the Inspector General, n.d.). Throughout the evaluation process, inspectors general build the capacity of subordinate organizations to evaluate their programs and to be proactive in utilizing evaluation
findings for program improvement. During inspector general site visits, it
is not the purpose of the inspector general to catch people red-handed in
program violations, but to check the status of a program and offer assistance
in its improvement.

AIGs have a dual organizational hierarchy, whereby they work with the
commander and staff in their threefold mission while at the same time
reporting to the Inspector General of the Army (commonly referred to as
the TIG). Interactions with both entities include in-person site visits, data
and trend meta-analyses, and regular status reports and presentations. This
dual reporting structure acts "as checks and balances on the objectivity of
the evaluators" (Sonnichsen, 1989, p. 60), thus providing a structured qual-
ity-control mechanism, and a balance between conducting evaluations and
building evaluation capacity.

Internal evaluators in other small organizations should take on a teaching and training focus in all they do. Once trained in evaluation, internal
evaluators have the responsibility to train others. This training is often one-
on-one but can effectively be extended to different sized groups. Training
topics may range from those that build technical skills specific to evaluation, such as skills in needs assessment, data collection, and analysis, to
organizational development skills that help to build an evaluation mind-set,
such as skills in planning, communication, and conflict resolution.

NEW DIRECTIONS FOR EVALUATION • DOI: 10.1002/ev

Seasoned Capacity: Fostering Evaluation Proliferation

At the seasoned level of evaluation capacity, the organizational conditions, process factors, and outcomes are clearly and distinctly present in the day-to-day organizational functions (Lyle, 2000; Sonnichsen, 2000). The organization has greater flexibility in what and how it evaluates. Human resources are sufficient not only to perform evaluation, but to perpetuate its use. The organizational hierarchy distinctively links the internal evaluators with executive staff members. Internal evaluators have the knowledge, skills, attitudes, and abilities to handle political, social, and administrative situations that may arise during the course of evaluation. Evaluation terminology, significance, and mind-set are firmly implanted throughout the organization. Evaluation is something sought after rather than avoided (Preskill, 2008).

During the time I spent as an inspector general, the evaluation capacity of much of the organization increased immensely, to include technical training in evaluating a given topic, actively putting systems and structures in place to promote evaluation (e.g., an evaluation help line and training key leaders), and building a proactive, immersive experience integrated throughout the program evaluations. The AIG became a consistent promoter of *advocacy evaluation* (Sonnichsen, 1987), which is an integral part of internal evaluation encompassing "the active involvement of evaluators and their supervisors in the organizational process of discussion, approval, and implementation of recommendations after the completion of the evaluation" (Sonnichsen, 1987, p. 35). The evaluation team actively promoted the evaluation process and evaluation capacity-building opportunities throughout the region.

I do not want to leave readers with the impression that my experience with the AIG was an ideal situation—far from it. Like most organizations, the AIG still had many political, logistical, economic, and social challenges to evaluation that will likely take quite some time to overcome. Nevertheless, the organization did make great strides in developing and internalizing evaluation capacity, which the purpose of this article highlights.

At the seasoned level, internal evaluators in small organizations can actively propagate evaluation to the degree that it becomes a habitual process. Programs are evaluated in the developmental, formative, and summative stages. Evaluation processes and results are used for mission development, vision creation, and strategy decision making. Employees at all levels are thinking evaluatively as they run their respective programs. The internal evaluator regularly engages members of the organization in training as well as in conducting evaluations. Evaluation capacity becomes engrained in the very fiber of the organization.

Evaluating Capacity-Building Efforts

There have been some discussions in evaluation journals (e.g., *The American Journal of Evaluation, New Directions for Evaluation*), online forums

NEW DIRECTIONS FOR EVALUATION • DOI: 10.1002/ev

(e.g., EVALTALK), conferences, and informal settings on how to evaluate capacity-building efforts, and those discussions warrant some attention here in this article. The ECB process is similar in nature to formative evaluation efforts. I use the term *formative* because of the ongoing nature of evaluation capacity building (Preskill & Boyle, 2008) and the foci of the internal evaluator (Clifford & Sherman, 1983). There are still evaluation questions, methods, criteria, standards, time lines, results, recommendations, and other areas to take into consideration. The specifics, of course, differ depending on the evaluand (as with any evaluation).

A Checklist for Building Organizational Evaluation Capacity (Volkov & King, 2007) and the Institutionalizing Evaluation Checklist (Stufflebeam, 2002) have been created to guide evaluators and organizations in understanding the breadth and depth of evaluation capacity-building efforts and in making adjustments as necessary. These checklists discuss such areas as organizational context, ECB structures, resources, communications, and personnel. Internal evaluators may use these checklists or other tools as guides to assessing and increasing the capacity of their organization to subscribe to and implement evaluation in their day-to-day activities. With limited resources, small organizations need reliable and comprehensive frameworks they can look to for useful direction. Checklists provide frameworks that may readily be adapted to the size and scope of the organization or respective evaluation topic (Bamberger, Rugh, Church, & Fort, 2004).

Keys to Success of Capacity Building by an Internal Evaluator in a Small Organization

Along with the experiences of internal evaluation discussed previously, there are some key takeaways that internal evaluators need to stay in tune with and be proactive in implementing. By following the principles described below, internal evaluators can minimize complacency or adverse feelings toward evaluation that often stem from misinformation.

Remain Committed to Evaluation

Internal evaluators frequently perform evaluation as only one of several professional duties. For example, an elementary school may designate a teacher to conduct a formative evaluation of science, technology, engineering, and mathematics (STEM) education progress in that school (Huffman, Lawrenz, Thomas, & Clarkson, 2006). The individual must balance evaluation responsibilities with other duties (e.g., planning lessons, meeting with parents, staff meetings). One key is to remain committed to evaluation while continuing to move the organization forward in its strategic goals (Clifford & Sherman, 1983; Love, 1983). In the absence of commitment, evaluation and capacity building will be overshadowed by other duties and responsibilities. If the internal evaluator understands the benefit and priority of evaluation, that evaluator will take the necessary steps to ensure evaluations and associated capacity-building activities are ongoing within the organization. The internal evaluator can accomplish this by understanding the position of all the stakeholders involved and being attentive to their needs. The internal evaluator can also lend an objective viewpoint and raise an evaluative voice in the areas of designing an appropriate evaluation and using evaluation results.

Within the office of the AIG, of primary concern was the elimination of bias in favor of certain departments or subgroups within the organization (Mangano, 1992). It may seem easy to some members of the organization to take advantage of the technical assistance role of the inspector general in gaining favoritism. For example, as the inspector general provides technical assistance on a given subject, there may be the temptation to ask the inspector general to upgrade the evaluation results regardless of the newfound subject knowledge. However, the inspector general has a specific duty to evaluate and report the status of a given program or process in an unbiased manner. Inspectors general keep technical assistance or other aid separate from the evaluation results for that very reason. For example, after describing the results of the evaluation itself, the AIG may offer technical assistance by recommending the review of applicable regulations governing the evaluand, or referring the organization to points of contact who can provide subject-matter expertise for the evaluand.

Likewise, in other small organizations, internal evaluators must keep that separation between the program evaluation and any technical or informational assistance provided to staff members. This may be done by establishing a sequential separation between the two events, and a physical separation of the documentation of the events. In doing so, the internal evaluator can offer evaluation objectivity, and still maintain trust within the organization.

Balance the Development of Organizational and Evaluative Skills

A large part of evaluation capacity-building work involves creating a mindset conducive to evaluation. Although it is important for the internal evaluator to train the organization for technical skills related to evaluation, part of the capacity-building process involves organizational development.

Within the office of the AIG, inspectors general actively taught staff members during site visits how to review records, compute program statistics, or discuss program status with others in the organization. Inspectors general also taught organizational development techniques to ensure that programs purposefully feed into organizational missions, and that the organization is able to prove program viability and livelihood. For example, because one of the primary missions of a maintenance unit is to ensure that all vehicles are licensed and in working order, the vehicle licensing program and its associated evaluation should be a high priority. As organizational and evaluative skills work in tandem, members of other small organizations may

NEW DIRECTIONS FOR EVALUATION • DOI: 10.1002/ev

more frequently turn to the internal evaluator for technical assistance and may be more proactive in resolving program difficulties.

Maintain Essential Evaluation Competencies

The Competence section of the *Guiding Principles for Evaluators* (Newman, Scheirer, Shadish, & Wye, 1995) advises evaluators to "possess the education, abilities, skills, and experience appropriate to undertake the tasks proposed in the evaluation," and to "continually seek to maintain and improve their competencies in order to provide the highest level of performance in their evaluations" (p. 22–23). This applies to internal evaluators as well as external ones. Such competencies may include "train[ing] others involved in conducting the evaluation, pursu[ing] professional development in evaluation, and facilitat[ing] constructive interpersonal interaction" (Stevahn, King, Ghere, & Minnema, 2005, p. 51). As the evaluation office builds its own evaluation competencies, doing so aids that office in developing a positive reputation with other members of the organization, and those people will be more open to future evaluations and capacity-building efforts.

Within the offices of the AIG, all new inspectors general must complete a full-time, 3-week course at the AIG headquarters before they may be allowed to perform the duties of an inspector general. This course includes lecture and application activities surrounding the three major functions of the inspector general (i.e., inspections, assistance, and investigations), as well as military-specific issues (e.g., wartime functions, intelligence oversight, joint task forces) (Office of the Inspector General, n.d.). Refresher courses and other professional development opportunities (e.g., conferences) are required of all inspectors general in order for them to keep abreast of new developments in the field and to improve their professional skill sets continually.

Although resources may be limited, internal evaluators in small organizations can utilize multiple approaches when it comes to evaluation training. Training classes, workshops, seminars, and discussions, in both synchronous and asynchronous mode, are now abundant in the evaluation field. Internal evaluators may take advantage of these and other opportunities to build their own skills, as well as include members of their organization in such training or at least share the acquired knowledge with them, as appropriate.

Focus on Evaluation Processes and Relevance

Internal evaluators must also focus on performing specific evaluations and understanding how those evaluations fit in with the broader picture of organizational development. For example, within the offices of the AIG, evaluators sought to see both "the trees and the forest" when carrying out evaluative activities. In coordination with the Commanding General and other senior staff, the AIG selects timely and relevant evaluation topics of concern to all parties involved. Many topics are chosen based on changes in regulations governing particular programs (e.g., new requirements for medical records documentation), performance levels (e.g., areas in need of improvement in the Army Physical Fitness Program), or evidence of fraud, waste, and abuse (e.g., related to vehicle licensing).

Internal evaluators in small organizations must also focus on the implications of evaluation. "The evaluator must be a critical thinker and not just a technician" (House, 1988, p. 45). Rather than be simply numbers crunchers, internal evaluators must also be the eyes and ears of the organization. Internal evaluators can report the evaluation results and make recommendations to direct program needs—linking those programs back to the organizational mission. The internal evaluator, who sees the big picture as well as the details, can generate and integrate evaluation information when and where the information is needed most. The Commanding General and senior staff directly and actively use inspection results for course correction, program development, and assistance training (Sonnichsen, 1989). Inspectors general and auditors share the results with each other not only to avoid duplication of effort, but to inform and improve upon ongoing and future audits and evaluations.

Conclusion

Building evaluation capacity is crucial for internal evaluators and is the very process of internal evaluation. Building capacity allows for proliferating the importance of evaluation throughout the organization "thus becoming a social epidemic by focusing on what and how people learn from and about evaluation" (Preskill, 2008, p. 127). As internal evaluators demonstrate evaluation benefits, train members of the organization in evaluation principles and techniques, and use other, earlier described, ways to institutionalize evaluation, evaluation capacity will be increasingly integrated into organizational mission, goals, and activities.

Building evaluation capacity promotes self-sufficiency within an organization. Whether in government (Mackay, 2002), education (Huffman et al., 2006), or other areas, evaluation capacity helps the organization to think evaluatively and to access evaluation resources. In these lean economic times, training and evaluation are often among the first line items to be cut—often at the expense of program visibility. Building evaluation capacity helps to minimize the effects of such budget cuts by providing organizations with inside expertise in evaluation such that they still are able to assess their activities regardless of the economic situation.

Building evaluation capacity should contribute to developing organizational culture and cohesion. Hoole (2008) stated, "When a learning culture develops and organizational learning occurs, the opportunity for increased effectiveness abounds" (p. 95). Likewise, King (2002, 2005) helps evaluators understand the plethora of situations where an evaluative learning culture can bring increased unity and deeper relationships on key organizational issues. Building relationships helps the internal evaluator to develop credibility as an evaluator and serves as a catalyst for potentially smoother evaluation processes.

This article not only brings the struggles of the internal evaluator to the forefront, but also provides insight into potential solutions to those struggles. Although few issues are easily resolved, evaluators can document the evaluation environment, the issues faced by the organization (e.g., evaluative, social, political, organizational), the solutions undertaken, and the results of those courses of action in order to understand more fully how to deal with internal evaluation issues. The evaluator may thus have these scenarios at his or her disposal for references in resolving future issues.

Thus, I extend the call to other evaluators to expand the research in this area of evaluation in two critical areas: documenting the development of evaluation capacity itself, and documenting the feelings, attitudes, and experiences of those undergoing evaluation capacity development. Doing this will help to expand the pool of best practices so that other organizations may emulate such an endeavor.

References

Baizerman, M., Compton, D. W., & Stockdill, S. H. (2002). New directions for ECB. *New Directions for Evaluation, 93*, 109–120.

Bamberger, M., Rugh, J., Church, M., & Fort, L. (2004). Shoestring evaluation: Designing impact evaluations under budget, time and data constraints. *American Journal of Evaluation, 25*(1), 5–37. doi:10.1177/109821400402500102

Clifford, D. L., & Sherman, P. (1983). Internal evaluation: Integrating program evaluation and management. *New Directions for Program Evaluation, 20*, 23–45.

Compton, D. W., & Baizerman, M. (2007). Defining evaluation capacity building. *American Journal of Evaluation, 28*(1), 118–119.

Cummings, O. W., Nowakowski, J. R., Schwandt, T. A., Eichelberger, R. T., Kleist, K. C., Larson, C. L., et al. (1988). Business perspectives on internal/external evaluation. *New Directions for Program Evaluation, 39*, 59–74.

Duffy, B. P. (1994). Use and abuse of internal evaluation. *New Directions for Program Evaluation, 64*, 25–32.

Duignan, P. (2003). Mainstreaming evaluation or building evaluation capability? Three key elements. *New Directions for Evaluation, 99*, 7–21.

Hoole, E., & Patterson, T. E. (2008). Voices from the field: Evaluation as part of a learning culture. *New Directions for Evaluation, 2008*(119), 93–113. doi:10.1002/ev.270

House, E. (1989). Response to Richard Sonnichsen. *American Journal of Evaluation, 10*(3), 64–65.

House, E. R. (1986). Internal evaluation. *American Journal of Evaluation, 7*(1), 63–64.

House, E. R. (1988). Evaluating the FBI: A response to Sonnichsen. *American Journal of Evaluation, 9*(3), 43–46.

Huffman, D., Lawrenz, F., Thomas, K., & Clarkson, L. (2006). Collaborative evaluation communities in urban schools: A model of evaluation capacity building for STEM education. *New Directions for Evaluation, 109*, 73–85.

King, J. A. (2002). Building the evaluation capacity of a school district. *New Directions for Evaluation, 93*, 63–80. doi: 10.1002/ev.42

King, J. A. (2005). A proposal to build evaluation capacity at the Bunche–Da Vinci Learning Partnership Academy. *New Directions for Evaluation, 106*, 85–97. doi: 10.1002/ev.153

King, J. A. (2007). Developing evaluation capacity through process use. *New Directions for Evaluation, 116*, 45–59.

Lambur, M. T. (2008). Organizational structures that support internal program evaluation. *New Directions for Evaluation, 120*, 41–54.

Love, A. J. (Ed.). (1983, Winter). Developing effective internal evaluation [Special issue]. *New Directions for Program Evaluation, 20*.

Lyle, C. G. (2000). Book review: High impact internal evaluation. *American Journal of Evaluation, 21*(2), 285–288.

Mackay, K. (2002). The World Bank's ECB experience. *New Directions for Evaluation, 93*, 81–100. doi: 10.1002/ev.43

Mangano, M. F. (1992). The inspectors general. *New Directions for Program Evaluation, 55*, 57–63.

Morell, J. A. (2000). Internal evaluation: A synthesis of traditional methods and industrial engineering. *American Journal of Evaluation, 21*(1), 41–52.

Nevo, D. (1993). The evaluation-minded school: An application of perceptions from program evaluation 1. *American Journal of Evaluation, 14*(1), 39–47.

Newcomer, K. E. (2004). How might we strengthen evaluation capacity to manage evaluation contracts? *American Journal of Evaluation, 25*(2), 209–218.

Newman, D. L., Scheirer, M. A., Shadish, W. R., & Wye, C. (1995). Guiding principles for evaluators. *New Directions for Program Evaluation, 66*, 19–26.

Newman, F. L., Heverly, M. A., Rosen, M., Kopta, S. M., & Bedell, R. (1983). Influences on internal evaluation data dependability: Clinicians as a source of variance. *New Directions for Program Evaluation, 20*, 71–92.

Nowakowski, A. C. (1989). Strategy for internal evaluators. *New Directions for Program Evaluation, 44*, 45–57.

Office of the Inspector General (n.d.). Retrieved from: http://wwwpublic.ignet.army.mil/

Preskill, H. (2008). Evaluation's second act: A spotlight on learning. *American Journal of Evaluation, 29*(2), 127–138.

Preskill, H., & Boyle, S. (2008). A multidisciplinary model of evaluation capacity building. *American Journal of Evaluation, 29*(4), 443–459.

Smith, C. L., & Freeman, R. L. (2002). Using continuous system level assessment to build school capacity. *American Journal of Evaluation, 23*(3), 307–319.

Sonnichsen, D. (1989). Letters. *American Journal of Evaluation, 10*(3), 59–63.

Sonnichsen, R. C. (1987). An internal evaluator responds to Ernest House's views on internal evaluation. *American Journal of Evaluation, 8*(4), 34–36.

Sonnichsen, R. C. (1990). Another view of program inspections by the offices of inspectors general. *New Directions for Program Evaluation, 48*, 77–86.

Sonnichsen, R. C. (2000). *High impact internal evaluation: A practitioner's guide to evaluating and consulting inside organizations*. Thousand Oaks, CA: Sage.

Sporn, D. L. (1989). A conversation with Richard C. Sonnichsen. *American Journal of Evaluation, 10*(2), 63–67.

Stevahn, L., King, J. A., Ghere, G., & Minnema, J. (2005). Establishing essential competencies for program evaluators. *American Journal of Evaluation, 26*(1), 43–59.

Stockdill, S. H., Baizerman, M., & Compton, D. W. (2002). Toward a definition of the ECB process: A conversation with the ECB literature. *New Directions for Evaluation, 93*, 7–26.

Stufflebeam, D. L. (2002). *Institutionalizing evaluation checklist*. Retrieved from http://www.wmich.edu/evalctr/checklists/institutionalizingeval.pdf

Taut, S. (2007). Defining evaluation capacity building: Utility considerations. *American Journal of Evaluation, 28*(1), 120.

Taylor-Powell, E., & Boyd, H. H. (2008). Evaluation capacity building in complex organizations. *New Directions for Evaluation, 120,* 55–69.

The Evaluation Center. (n.d.). *Glossary of evaluation terms.* Retrieved from http://ec.wmich.edu/glossary/prog-glossary.htf#G-I

Volkov, B. B., & King, J. A. (2007). *A checklist for building organizational evaluation capacity.* Retrieved from http://www.wmich.edu/evalctr/checklists/ecb.pdf

Whitney, D. K., & Trosten-Bloom, A. (2003). *The power of appreciative inquiry: A practical guide to positive change.* San Francisco, CA: Berrett-Koehler.

Wye, C., & Sonnichsen, R. (1992). Another look at the future of program evaluation in the federal government: Five views. *American Journal of Evaluation, 13*(3), 185–195.

MICHELLE E. BARON is an independent evaluation strategist based in Arlington, Virginia.

Volkov, B. B., & Baron, M. E. (2011). Issues in internal evaluation: Implications for practice, training, and research. In B. B. Volkov & M. E. Baron (Eds.), *Internal evaluation in the 21st century. New Directions for Evaluation, 132,* 101–111.

8

Issues in Internal Evaluation: Implications for Practice, Training, and Research

Boris B. Volkov, Michelle E. Baron

Abstract

This chapter highlights themes running throughout the preceding chapters and illustrates important issues in improving the design, implementation, and use of internal evaluation. The authors contemplate where internal evaluation might go in the future by suggesting new directions for how internal evaluation is conceptualized and practiced to realize its potential for enhancing the organizational and program growth and competitive advantage. © Wiley Periodicals, Inc., and the American Evaluation Association.

Most, if not all, organizations and programs have ineffective, underachieving, and even broken strategies and processes that need to be rectified. It is one of the reasons why the GPRA Modernization Act of 2010 prescribed a new role for the Office of Management and Budget (OMB): the responsibility to assess program performance; inform the agency, the Congress, and the Government Accountability Office of unmet goals; and prepare plans to correct performance deficiencies. Evaluation is accentuated as a central aspect for performance management, and identifying key skills and competencies for evaluating programs is the new requirement that is expected to have a lasting impact on federal evaluation functions. Earlier in this issue, Sandra Mathison points out that an emphasis on performance measurement will continue and that evaluation will strive to narrow the gap between performance measurement and programmatic decision making. For the internal evaluator, it becomes imperative to work with stakeholders and decision makers to make evaluation data more useful. With such tools and technologies as logic modeling, data visualization, and streamlined reporting strategies, internal evaluators should be able to get to the heart of what evaluation and performance measurement mean to organizational leaders and make it easier for decision makers to access that data for strategic and tactical purposes.

Boris Volkov suggests a grounded definition of internal evaluation as a comprehensive and context-dependent system of intraorganizational processes and resources for implementing and promoting evaluation activities. The main purposes of this system include generating credible and practical knowledge to inform decision making, make judgments about and improve programs and policies, and influence organizational learning and decision-making behavior. Through reliable evaluative research, advocacy, and decision-making support, the internal evaluation office should provide leadership on evaluation-related issues and influence organizational policies and practices. Within governmental settings, for example, the American Evaluation Association has launched *An Evaluation Roadmap for a More Effective Government* (2010), which among other recommendations, advises evaluators to "consult closely with Congress and non-federal stakeholders in defining program and policy objectives and critical operations and definitions of success" (p. 5). This notion of working together in a collaborative environment toward policy progress emphasizes the context-dependent nature of evaluation Volkov describes.

Internal evaluation practices in many organizations and programs have yet to live up to their potential. As Arnold Love indicates in his interview, the pure vision of Wildavsky's "self-evaluating organization" has not been fully actualized. Nevertheless, it has evolved significantly, and many evaluation practitioners and theorists are engaged in this developmental process. We are witness to the developing of a new style of internal evaluation, with its practitioners becoming much more proactive and creative in their involvement in their organization's processes to be able to reinforce their ability to create positive change on multiple levels. Fetterman (1998) asserts that "[p]opulations shift, goals shift, knowledge about program practices and their values change, and external forces are highly unstable. By internalizing and institutionalizing self-evaluation processes and practices, a dynamic and responsive approach to evaluation can be developed to accommodate these shifts" (p. 382). Reflective of Patton's concept of developmental evaluation, evaluators and organizations must work in concert to "make sense of what emerges under conditions of complexity, documenting and interpreting the dynamics, interactions, and interdependencies that occur as innovations unfold" (Patton, 2010, p. 7).

Contextual Factors

Even though evaluation's role is paramount for ensuring program success, many organizations, both for- and nonprofits, struggle to fund external evaluations. One of the strategies for overcoming this barrier is increasing an organization's internal capacity to design, implement, and manage effective evaluation projects. This capacity in organizations may become a function of an internal evaluation unit consisting of full- or part-time employees. By developing and sustaining a robust internal evaluation function, organizations will demonstrate "a willingness, perhaps even a desire, to find out how well programs have done and in what ways they could do better next time" (Chelimsky, 2001, p. 23). Such a desire is not a given fact, both unfortunately and unsurprisingly. Evaluation's interface with organizational practices and decision making is largely affected by the organizational climate. According to Brazil (1999), organizational cultures, including approaches to management, range from being exploitative–authoritarian to consultative–participatory. The latter is the best culture for the effective evaluation practice through its using evaluations for informing decisions and actions as opposed to penalizing subordinates. Sanders (2002) states that

> The problem of developing an evaluation culture in organizations remains perplexing. Organizations talk about it and say they want it, but evaluation frequently becomes a secondary activity, appearing when there is pressure, problems, or mandates. For those of us who are true believers in the benefits of evaluation, the question of what we can do to make it part of the everyday life of organizations remains unanswered. (p. 253)

There are other multiple constraints related to the proper functioning of internal evaluation, including a notoriously common financial barrier. For example, according to King and Rohmer-Hirt, American public education faces the challenge of securing resources to sustain meaningful evaluation efforts in response to the demands of accountability and increasing student achievement. Because of the lack of funding, evaluation departments may be unable to evaluate many programs routinely, and forced to shift from entitlement allocations to competitive grants, whereby internal evaluators must navigate through external networks to secure programmatic funding and other nonmonetary support.

Illuminating his experiences as the chief of evaluation for public diplomacy at the U.S. Department of State, Ted Kniker introduces us to the key successes and pitfalls of internal evaluation in federal government based upon the trends toward performance and results analysis, discussion, and reporting. The author describes the multiple "ills" of internal evaluation: the lack of will (lack of a clear value proposition and leadership support for internal evaluation); the lack of skill (common problems agencies have in getting the right expertise in evaluation); the lack of bills (appropriate resources for evaluation); the lack of fill (data-related issues); and evaluation kill (evaluation shelf-life [sits on the shelf] or half-life [too radioactive to release]). Effective internal and external communication was one key way that Kniker and his colleagues navigated these challenges, along with establishing a "collaborative, partnership-oriented relationship" among program managers and other stakeholders.

Organizations and their programs typically have unique goals, activities, and contextual conditions that create a need for different evaluation philosophies, missions, and approaches. In different organizations, internal evaluation embodies a wide range of activities to measure program effectiveness, inform decision making, improve programs, and contribute to organizational development. Dabelstein (2003) states that, when designing internal evaluation systems, it is necessary to take into account the specific government and administrative culture in the organization. Formal policies, systems, and practices are important; however, the effect of informal practices, symbolic actions, evaluative beliefs, values, and attitudes need to be considered, too (Davidson, 2001; McDonald, Rogers, & Kefford, 2003). In the decision-making process itself, "[o]ptions, effects, and consequences are rarely clear, and the decisionmaker may not always choose the most desirable option" according to Sonnichsen (2000, p. 122). In her chapter, Michelle Baron states that "[o]rganizations' exposure to evaluation may be limited depending on the background and experience of the employees and leadership of the organization, the priority of evaluation within the goals of the organization, and the access to evaluation training and expertise." Thus, it behooves evaluators to create instances and situations whereby organizations are exposed to various evaluation principles, concepts, and scenarios. As organizational exposure to evaluation increases, so also may grow within them an adherence to and even desire for those techniques designed for self-improvement.

Situational Responsiveness

Good understanding of and engagement with an organization's internal and external contexts are, therefore, imperative for IE professionals. There are no easy answers to many perplexing organizational problems, and there are no one-size-fits-all solutions. Internal evaluation is not a static system; it is an ongoing, developmental process. It means that internal evaluators should not rely blindly on the same timeworn, ostensibly gold-standard, analytical and information-gathering approaches, techniques, and associated assumptions. The best practices for internal evaluation should include "situational responsiveness" and "methodological appropriateness" (see Patton, 2008, p. 421).

The principle of methodological appropriateness signals to evaluators the need to be open-minded when investigating evaluation questions—selecting the methods (quantitative, qualitative, or mixed) that will most effectively answer the questions stakeholders want and need to know. Although the quantitative–qualitative debate has endured for decades, what pundits can agree on is the need for appropriate rationale in methodological selection and use. Donaldson, Christie, and Mark (2008) emphasize the need for focus on the goal of solving evaluation problems as the driving force in appropriate methodology:

> Simply stated, evaluators work with stakeholders to develop a common understanding of how a program is presumed to solve the problem(s) of interest; to formulate and prioritize key evaluation questions; and then to decide how best to gather credible evidence to answer those questions within practical, time, and resource constraints. This practical program evaluation approach is essentially method neutral within the broad domain of social science methodology. The focus on development of program theory and evaluation questions frees evaluators initially from having to presuppose use of one evaluation design or another. (p. 243)

The principle of situational responsiveness is in line with what Love (2005) describes as important trends in the practice of internal evaluation: monitoring systems to identify targets for in-depth evaluations; small program-level databases and distributed networks with rapid access to information and a quick response to changing needs; better reporting formats designed to provide concise, time-sensitive information; and engaging managers, staff, and clients in defining outcomes and developing measurement tools.

The last trend is supported by the King and Rohmer-Hirt account of the evaluative activity at the school level, which takes a form of participatory school improvement activities (e.g., data-based decision making, professional learning communities, teacher research, and collaborative action research). Use of professional learning communities with groups of teachers designing research efforts can beneficially complement internal evaluation efforts.

Use of Information Technology

High-impact evaluation necessitates high-quality information systems. At the same time, the design and maintenance of effective information and monitoring systems, quick-response databases and networks, and efficient and time-sensitive reporting mechanisms will increasingly rely on the information technology (IT). Undeniably, internal evaluation is entering a new era due to the rapid development of information technology, according to Mathison. Development and maintenance of electronic databases, information management systems, data warehousing, and the strategies for their mining become part of internal evaluator responsibilities. Governmental e-service delivery plans and open engagement tactics also call for new evaluation approaches and techniques. In this new digital governance era, Mathison goes on, "the fundamental idea of disaggregation in NPM [New Public Management] will necessarily give way to recentralization through information systems." Kniker and his evaluation unit developed their own online performance measurement and evaluation system (a combination between a survey tool, dashboard system, and report writer) to provide timely feedback to program managers. King and Rohmer-Hirt also tell us that "powerful developments in available technology have increasingly enabled districts to collect, analyze, and use assessment data to support individual student learning."

Expanding Roles

Francis Schweigert asserts that the internal evaluator's role is regulative as opposed to being productive (programming and results) or directive (as is management's). He sees the promise of the internal evaluator's unique role in viewing the organization and its programs with the insider's insight and at the same time taking a deliberate stand on objectivity: an "impartial spectator" (Smith, 1790/1984) with a "view from nowhere" (Nagel, 1986).

An emerging phenomenon in the program-evaluation field and academic literature is the multiplicity and elasticity of roles of the evaluation professionals, particularly internal evaluators. Volkov's analysis of the literature suggests a list of the essential, macrolevel roles, driving the evaluation function in the organizations. The categories of the most frequently cited evaluator roles include the following: change agent, educator about evaluation, ECB practitioner, (management) decision-making supporter, consultant, researcher/technical expert, advocate, and organizational learning supporter. New roles are also emerging, such as "the interpreters and translators between stakeholders and program managers, between researchers and practitioners, between politicals and careerists," as Kniker notes. How all these roles are realized is contingent on the evaluator's attitudes, knowledge, and skills, as well as a confluence of enabling contextual factors.

New directions for internal evaluation include proper uses of the above roles, as well as further adaptation and reframing of the evaluator's role kit to fit complex demands of the modern organization and society. In fulfilling these roles the internal evaluator should be able to act as a catalyst for organizational self-reflection and higher-level learning. The role of the internal evaluator will progressively change and expand, and promoting evaluative thinking throughout the entire organization will constitute one of the highly challenging and gratifying roles for the internal evaluators.

When nurturing the spirit of evaluation inquiry in organizations, however, we should remember that overeager proselytization of evaluation can be self-defeating. For example, Dahler-Larsen (2006) cautions us that careless popularization of evaluation may be rather harmful and lead to trivialization of evaluation and evaluation fatigue:

. . . [P]opularization of evaluation, as well as commercialization and the promotion of evaluation through organizational procedures and management systems, may all contribute to codification of evaluation, that is, to a reduction of evaluation to a standardized and thus predictable set of algorithms. Codification means that the sequencing and form of the elements of an evaluation process conform to a given recipe. (p.154)

Ethical Issues

In contemplating problems with and opportunities for internal evaluation, House (1986) noted that "internal evaluation is not necessarily a worse situation; it is a different situation. And what we need are new ideas for dealing with it" (p. 64). Internal evaluation's ethical issues include some high degree of potentiality for career concerns and identification with administrators personally (and becoming the tool for the administration) that may negatively impact the objectivity of internal evaluators.

In his chapter, Francis Schweigert highlights a few unique ethical challenges the internal evaluator faces—related to organizational loyalty and the risk of isolation or corruption. He is concerned about "an added complication for internal evaluators: dual loyalty," specifically, "loyalty to the public in their fidelity to evaluation standards" and "loyalty to their organization of hire where they serve as a member of the staff." The internal evaluators play a part in "this scene of moral interdependence—carefully balanced and navigated as it is—with a professional obligation to meet a standard beyond moral approval: a standard of public trust and accountability."

What opportunities are available to solve or mitigate ethical issues encountered by internal evaluators? Chelimsky (2009) argues that strategies are needed for handling situations where there is a conflict between loyalty to the evaluator's agency and conformity with evaluation principles. One approach could be utilizing external evaluators in conflict-prone cases. She also believes that all stakeholders involved in the organization's evaluation should accept and respect the principle of evaluative independence as an essential value. Arnold Love suggests engaging external experts every so often to review a sample of internal evaluation studies and provide feedback about their quality and potential areas of bias. Having an evaluation steering committee is also beneficial. Most definitely, all that should go together with the constant application of the AEA program evaluation standards and ethical guidelines to the day-to-day evaluation.

Evaluator Credibility

Over the years, the internal evaluator has gone from being seen as a pawn in the hands of the organization's administrator, to an advocate, to a manager of evaluative information, to a motivator and change agent for performance improvement. Each of these episodes has lent itself to the development of evaluator credibility. Schweigert maintains that "[h]ere the ethical practice of evaluation must stand as the public's guardian of the credibility of evidence-based planning and policy; on this the credibility and authority of evaluation itself depends." Thus, the processes of planning for and conducting of evaluation themselves form a cycle of credibility. Baron describes evaluator accessibility as a key factor in building that credibility, in that relationships are established, learning takes place, and the evaluator is seen as an expert and a trainer for the organization. As the internal evaluator practices ethical evaluation, his or her trustworthiness and the ability to train others in evaluation increase.

Combining and balancing the roles of internal and external evaluation also seems to be an important element in achieving a credible evaluation. Promising is the approach making use of the collaborations that mix internal and external evaluation by dividing different evaluation projects and tasks (Conley-Tyler, 2005). Mathison in her chapter also supports the authors, recommending the development of complementary and mutually beneficial partnerships between internal and external evaluation professionals. Kniker explains that the evaluations conducted by independent, external third parties helped his office overcome the perception that evaluation was being used to cut programs for political reasons and also afforded additional practical training for the evaluation staff.

Evaluation Training

Amongst us there are many "accidental evaluators" (which is not a bad notion, of course), in other words, those who became internal evaluators because of a confluence of circumstances outside of their control and who usually lack formal coursework in evaluation. There are also those who have received formal training in evaluation methods but who lack practical knowledge about how real-world organizations and programs function or proper expertise in specialized areas of social programming. Love (1983) lamented that the formal training of evaluators left them unprepared for the uncertain world of internal evaluation. It is still the case today, according to Love ("Internal Evaluation a Quarter-Century Later," Volkov, this issue), whose "main concern is that most evaluators in general do not have a formal training in finance, in accounting, in budgeting . . . to be able to cost a process or an outcome." Mathison concurs by saying that one of the reasons that the expectation that cost-effectiveness would become a strong ingredient of program evaluation has never been fully realized is due to evaluators' lack of knowledge of the subject.

Kniker (this issue) would like to see internal evaluators have political savvy and communication skills, and be equally as good in project management, contract management, knowledge management, marketing, and public relations. We also think that it is useful for aspiring internal evaluators to understand how organizations and their economic and political environments work and interact. Consequently, future evaluation training in its multiple forms (academic courses, seminars, internships, etc.) should address those sensitive areas for internal evaluators. Morell (2000) sees such training as much "needed to build the common knowledge base and collective mind set that are needed to change the nature of intra-program evaluation activity" (p. 52).

Research on Internal Evaluation

As internal evaluation is progressively recognized as vital for organizational learning and development, the need for a rigorous research on its complex issues becomes of greater importance. There are a number of challenges in implementing internal evaluation in the intricate contexts of contemporary organizations, and at least some of them can be transformed into opportunities for research on this emergent discipline. What has definitely become evident is the complexity of internal evaluation as a system and practice, and there is a strong need for its clear conceptualization and operationalization.

Evaluation science should be further advanced to understand the complex dynamics of interrelationships between internal evaluation processes and organizations. One line for research could look into the mechanisms of acceptance of internal evaluation versus resistance to evaluation, and what internal and external factors work together to trigger those mechanisms in specific organizational contexts. For instance, Chelimsky (2009) is convinced that we need "strong, current information about problems and successes that evaluators are experiencing in their workplaces, and about which parts of the evaluation process are being affected by what political pressures" (p . 63). Christie (2008) stresses a need for a more detailed understanding of the notion of internal evaluators. We concur with her and suggest that one of the directions for research be identifying an appropriate, comprehensive set of competencies and skills required of a successful internal evaluator. The outcomes from such empirical work and evidence-based practice should be able to be translated into the most appropriate training models for internal evaluation contexts.

In conclusion, we would like to call for intensified efforts to advance scientific inquiry into the issues and challenges associated with this type of evaluation—with both researchers and communities of practice engaged in dialogue around the topics mentioned in this volume and beyond. The following are sample questions that may be explored in the coming months and years. How can internal evaluators effectively influence organizational climate to embrace evaluation? What new roles are capable of strengthening the probability for successful internal evaluation? What skills and competencies should support those roles and become part of evaluator training? How do the Guiding Principles and Joint Standards of Evaluation have unique meaning for the internal evaluator? How can ethical issues be resolved in complex, multistakeholder, politically charged internal environments? What rapid-response, evaluation data management systems and approaches are most sensible given resource constraints?

Keeping in mind that the internal evaluation literature is still rather limited, we are joining Sonnichsen's (2000) invitation for internal evaluators to "begin to record and publish their experiences, creating a literature, with not only innovative practical solutions and applications for employment inside organizations but also a theory of use that will contribute to increased acceptance and appreciation of the benefits of internal evaluation practice" (p. 302). It is our hope that the issues highlighted in this issue have found a receptive audience and the reader will come away with a better understanding of who/what the 21st-century internal evaluator is and how we can take the business of internal evaluation from ordinary to extraordinary.

References

American Evaluation Association. (2010). *An evaluation roadmap for a more effective government.* Retrieved from http://www.eval.org/EPTF.asp

Brazil, K. (1999). A framework for developing evaluation capacity in health care settings. *International Journal of Health Care Assurance, 10,* vi–xi.

Chelimsky, E. (2001). What evaluation could do to support foundations: A framework with nine component parts. *American Journal of Evaluation, 22*(1), 13–28.

Chelimsky, E. (2009). Integrating evaluation units into the political environment of government: The role of evaluation policy. *New Directions for Evaluation, 123,* 51–66.

Christie, C. A. (2008). Interview with Eric Barela. *American Journal of Evaluation, 29*(4), 534–546.

Conley-Tyler, M. (2005). A fundamental choice: Internal or external evaluation? *Evaluation Journal of Australasia, 4*(1/2), 3–11.

Dabelstein, N. (2003). Evaluation capacity development: Lessons learned. *Evaluation, 9*(3), 365–369.

Dahler-Larsen, P. (2006). Evaluation after disenchantment: Five issues shaping the role of evaluation in society. In I. F. Shaw, J. C. Greene, & M. M. Mark (Eds.), *The Sage handbook of evaluation.* London, United Kingdom: Sage.

Davidson E.J. (2001, November). *Mainstreaming evaluation into an organization's "Learning Culture."* Paper presented at the 2001 meeting of the American Evaluation Association, St. Louis, Mo.

Donaldson, S. I., Christie, C. A., & Mark, M. M. (2008). *What counts as credible evidence in applied research and evaluation practice?* Newbury Park, CA: Sage.

Fetterman, D. M. (1998). Empowerment evaluation and the Internet: A synergistic relationship. *Current Issues in Education, 1*(4).

House, E. R. (1986). Internal evaluation. *American Journal of Evaluation, 7*(1), 63–64.

Love, A. J. (1983). The organizational context and the development of internal evaluation. *New Directions for Program Evaluation, 20,* 5–22.

Love, A. J. (2005). Internal evaluation. In S. Mathison (Ed.), *Encyclopedia of evaluation* (pp. 206–207). Thousand Oaks, CA: Sage.

McDonald, B., Rogers, P., & Kefford, B. (2003). Teaching people to fish? Building the evaluation capability of public sector organizations. *Evaluation, 9*(1), 9–29.

Morell, J. A. (2000). Internal evaluation: A synthesis of traditional methods and industrial engineering. *American Journal of Evaluation, 21*(1), 41–52.

Nagel, T. (1986). *The view from nowhere.* New York, NY: Oxford University Press.

Patton, M. Q. (2008). *Utilization-focused evaluation.* Thousand Oaks, CA: Sage.

Patton, M. Q. (2010). *Developmental evaluation: Applying complexity concepts to enhance innovation and use.* New York, NY: The Guilford Press.

Sanders, J. R. (2002). A vision for evaluation. *American Journal of Evaluation, 23,* 253–259.

Smith, A. (1984). *The theory of moral sentiments* (D. D. Raphael & A. L. MacFie, Eds.; 6th ed.). Indianapolis, IN: Liberty Fund. (Original work published 1790)

Sonnichsen, R. C. (2000). *High impact internal evaluation: A practitioner's guide to evaluating and consulting inside organizations.* Thousand Oaks, CA: Sage.

BORIS B. VOLKOV is an assistant professor of evaluation studies with the Center for Rural Health and Department of Family and Community Medicine at the University of North Dakota School of Medicine and Health Sciences.

MICHELLE E. BARON is an independent evaluation strategist based in Arlington, Virginia.

INDEX

NEW DIRECTIONS FOR EVALUATION
ORDER FORM SUBSCRIPTION AND SINGLE ISSUES

DISCOUNTED BACK ISSUES:

Use this form to receive 20% off all back issues of *New Directions for Evaluation*.
All single issues priced at **$23.20** (normally $29.00)

TITLE	ISSUE NO.	ISBN

Call 888-378-2537 or see mailing instructions below. When calling, mention the promotional code JBNND to receive your discount. For a complete list of issues, please visit www.josseybass.com/go/ev

SUBSCRIPTIONS: (1 YEAR, 4 ISSUES)

☐ New Order   ☐ Renewal

U.S.	☐ Individual: $89	☐ Institutional: $295
CANADA/MEXICO	☐ Individual: $89	☐ Institutional: $335
ALL OTHERS	☐ Individual: $113	☐ Institutional: $369

Call 888-378-2537 or see mailing and pricing instructions below.
Online subscriptions are available at www.onlinelibrary.wiley.com

ORDER TOTALS:

Issue / Subscription Amount: $ _____

Shipping Amount: $ _____
(for single issues only – subscription prices include shipping)

Total Amount: $ _____

SHIPPING CHARGES:

First Item $6.00
Each Add'l Item $2.00

(No sales tax for U.S. subscriptions. Canadian residents, add GST for subscription orders. Individual rate subscriptions must be paid by personal check or credit card. Individual rate subscriptions may not be resold as library copies.)

BILLING & SHIPPING INFORMATION:

☐ **PAYMENT ENCLOSED:** *(U.S. check or money order only. All payments must be in U.S. dollars.)*

☐ **CREDIT CARD:**   ☐ VISA   ☐ MC   ☐ AMEX

Card number _____ Exp. Date _____

Card Holder Name _____ Card Issue # _____

Signature _____ Day Phone _____

☐ **BILL ME:** *(U.S. institutional orders only. Purchase order required.)*

Purchase order # _____
Federal Tax ID 13559302 • GST 89102-8052

Name _____

Address _____

Phone _____ E-mail _____

Copy or detach page and send to: **John Wiley & Sons, One Montgomery Street, Suite 1200, San Francisco, CA 94104-4594**

Order Form can also be faxed to: **888-481-2665**

PROMO JBNND